Street by Street

CHESTERFIELD

BOLSOVER, DRONFIELD, STAVELEY

Brimington, Clay Cross, Clowne, Grassmoor, Holmewood, Holymoorside, North Wingfield, Walton, Whittington, Wingerworth

1st edition May 2002

© Automobile Association Developments Limited 2002

 Ordnance Survey®

This product includes map data licensed from Ordnance Survey® with the permission of the Controller of Her Majesty's Stationery Office. © Crown copyright 2002. All rights reserved. Licence No: 399221.

Published by AA Publishing (a trading name of Automobile Association Developments Limited, whose registered office is Millstream, Maidenhead Road, Windsor, Berkshire SL4 5GD. Registered number 1878835).

The Post Office is a registered trademark of Post Office Ltd. in the UK and other countries.

Schools address data provided by Education Direct.

Mapping produced by the Cartographic Department of The Automobile Association. A00965

A CIP Catalogue record for this book is available from the British Library.

Printed by GRAFIASA S.A., Porto Portugal.

The contents of this atlas are believed to be correct at the time of the latest revision. However, the publishers cannot be held responsible for loss occasioned to any person acting or refraining from action as a result of any material in this atlas, nor for any errors, omissions or changes in such material. The publishers would welcome information to correct any errors or omissions and to keep this atlas up to date. Please write to Publishing, The Automobile Association, Fanum House (FH17), Basing View, Basingstoke, Hampshire, RG21 4EA.

Ref: ML196

Key to map pages — ii-iii

Key to map symbols — iv-1

Enlarged scale pages — 2-3

Street by Street — 4-43

Index – towns & villages — 44

Index – streets — 45-52

Index – featured places — 52-53

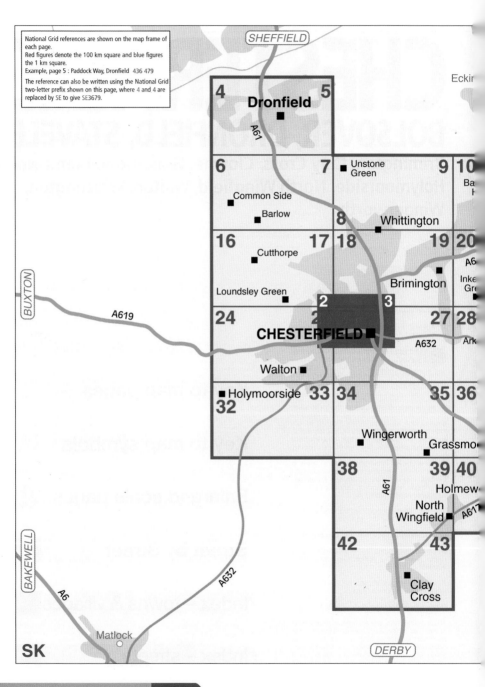

National Grid references are shown on the map frame of each page.
Red figures denote the 100 km square and blue figures the 1 km square.
Example, page 5 : Paddock Way, Dronfield 436 479

The reference can also be written using the National Grid two-letter prefix shown on this page, where 4 and 4 are replaced by SE to give SE3679.

SHEFFIELD

Eckir

4 **5**
Dronfield ■
A61

6 **7** Unstone Green ■ **9** **10**
Ba
H

Common Side ■
Barlow ■ **8** Whittington ■

16 **17** **18** **19** **20**
Cutthorpe ■ A6
Brimington ■ Inke Gre

Loundsley Green ■

BUXTON
A619 **2** **3**
24 **2** **27** **28**
CHESTERFIELD ■ A632 Ark

Walton ■

■ Holymoorside **33** **34** **35** **36**
32

Wingerworth ■ Grassmo

38 **39** **40**
A61 Holmew

North Wingfield ■ A61

BAKEWELL **42** **43**
A6 A632 Clay Cross ■

Matlock ○

SK DERBY

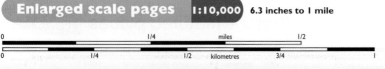

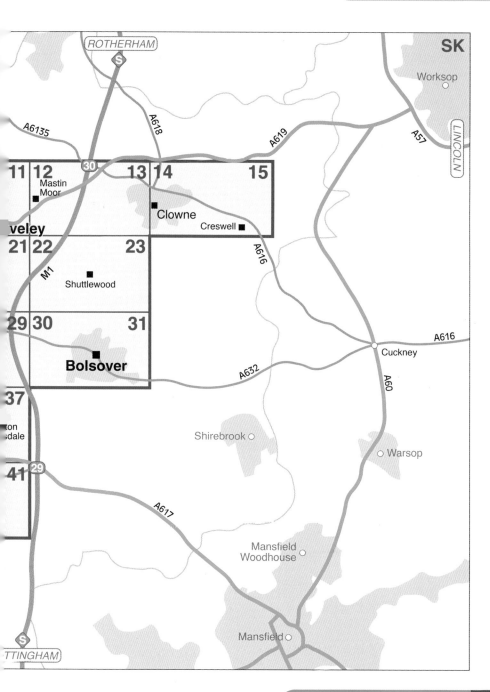

Junction 9	Motorway & junction	⊖	Underground station
Services	Motorway service area	⊖	Light Railway & station
	Primary road single/dual carriageway	+++++++++	Preserved private railway
Services	Primary road service area	LC	Level crossing
	A road single/dual carriageway	•—•—•—•—•	Tramway
	B road single/dual carriageway	- - - - - - - -	Ferry route
	Other road single/dual carriageway	....	Airport runway
	Minor/private road, access may be restricted	— · — · — · —	Boundaries - borough/district
← ←	One-way street	▼▼▼▼▼▼▼▼▼	Mounds
	Pedestrian area	93	Page continuation 1:15,000
============	Track or footpath	7	Page continuation to enlarged scale 1:10,000
	Road under construction		River/canal, lake, pier
⌐----⌐	Road tunnel		Aqueduct, lock, weir
AA	AA Service Centre	465 ▲ Winter Hill	Peak (with height in metres)
P	Parking		Beach
P+	Park & Ride		Coniferous woodland
	Bus/Coach station		Broadleaved woodland
	Railway & main railway station		Mixed woodland
	Railway & minor railway station		Park

	Cemetery	🎢	Theme Park
	Built-up area	⌂	Abbey, cathedral or priory
	Featured building	♜	Castle
⊓⊔⊓⊔⊓⊔	City wall	🏛	Historic house or building
A&E	24-hour Accident & Emergency hospital	Wakehurst Place NT	National Trust property
PO	Post Office	Ⓜ	Museum or art gallery
📖	Public library	🐎	Roman antiquity
i	Tourist Information Centre	⊥	Ancient site, battlefield or monument
⛽	Petrol station Major suppliers only	⛏	Industrial interest
†	Church/chapel	✺	Garden
🚻	Toilet	♣	Arboretum
♿	Toilet with disabled facilities	🛒	Farm or animal centre
PH	Public house AA recommended	🦌	Zoological or wildlife collection
🍴	Restaurant AA inspected	🦜	Bird collection
🎭	Theatre or performing arts centre	🦆	Nature reserve
🎦	Cinema	V	Visitor or heritage centre
⚑	Golf course	♔	Country park
▲	Camping AA inspected	◠	Cave
🚐	Caravan Site AA inspected	🌾	Windmill
▲🚐	Camping & Caravan Site AA inspected	🛢	Distillery, brewery or vineyard

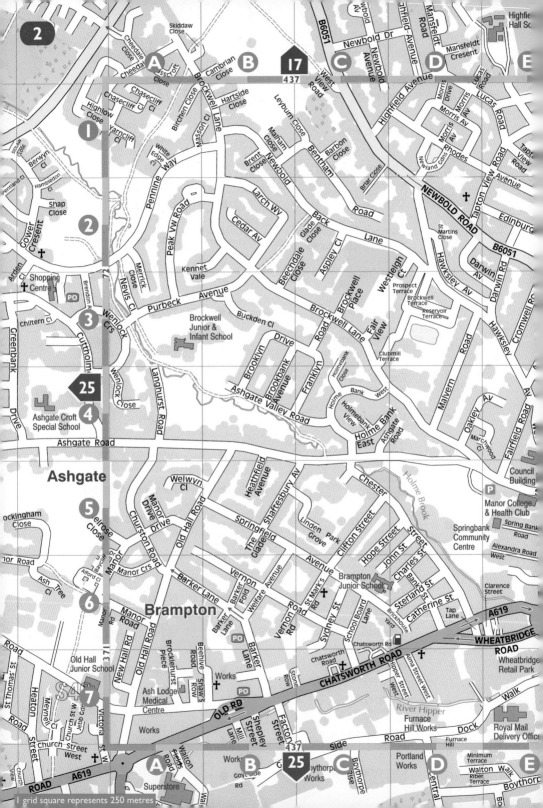

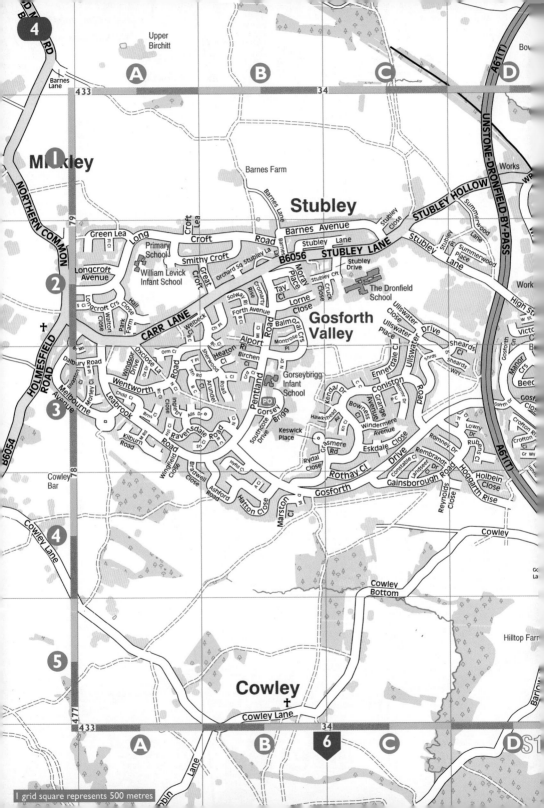

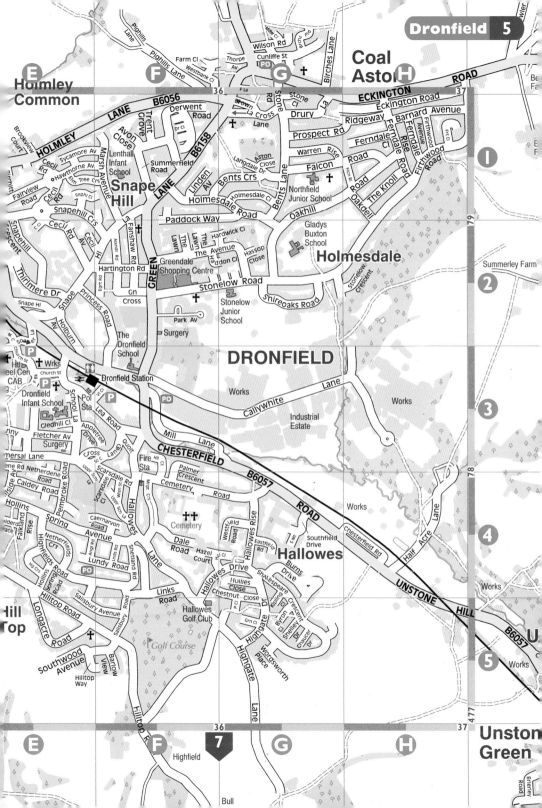

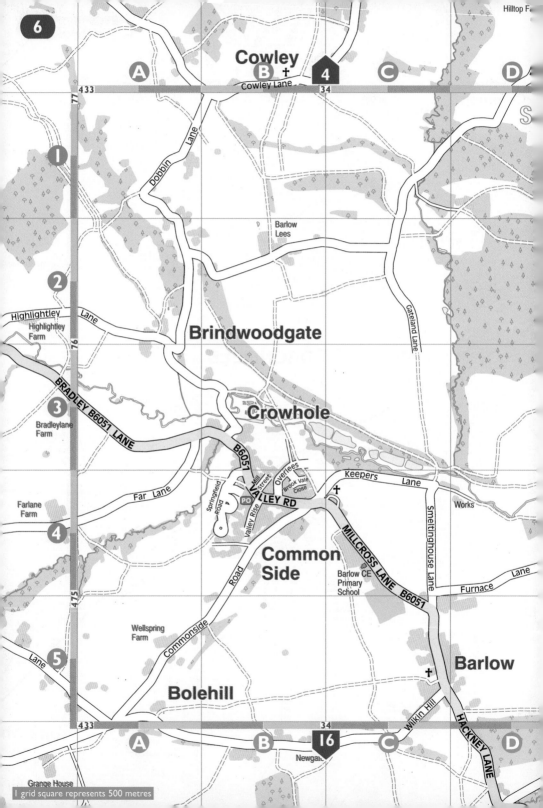

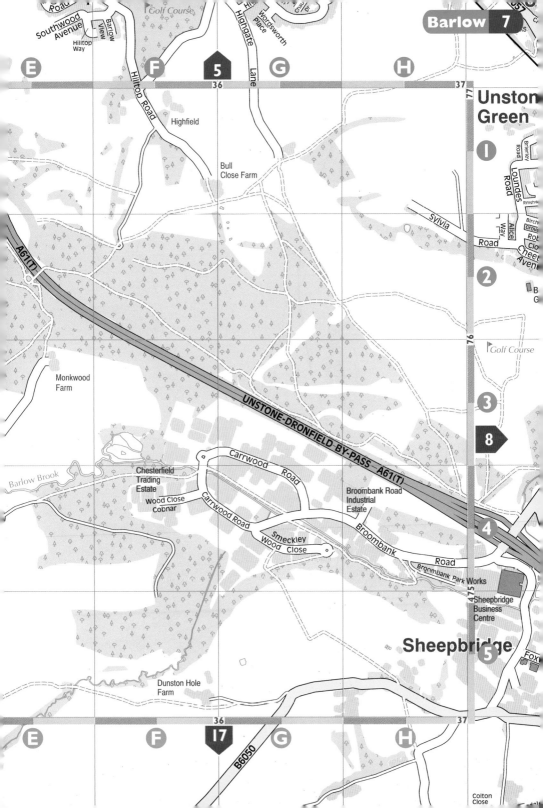

Golf Course

Southwood Avenue

Road

Barlow View

Hilltop Way

Hilltop Road

Highgate Lane

Wordsworth Place

E **F** 5 **G** **H**

36 37

Unston Green

Highfield

I

Bull Close Farm

Brierley Road

Loundes Road

Sylvia Road

Alice Way

Cheet Avenue

Birch Grove

Rob Clos

2

A61(T)

B G

77

76

Golf Course

Monkwood Farm

3

8

UNSTONE-DRONFIELD BY-PASS — A61(T)

Barlow Brook

Chesterfield Trading Estate

Carrwood Road

Broombank Road Industrial Estate

Wood Close

Cobnar

Carrwood Road

Smeckley Wood Close

Broombank Road

4

Broombank Park Works

75

Sheepbridge Business Centre

Dunston Hole Farm

Sheepbridge

5

Fox

E **F** 17 **G** **H**

36 37

B6050

Colton Close

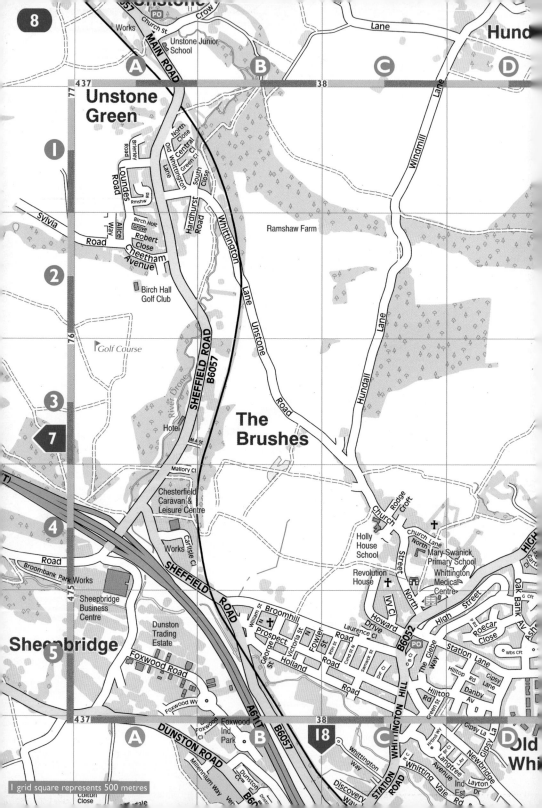

Staveley Lane

441
77

Nether Handley

1

Hagge Farm

A

B

42

C

White Lodge

D

2

Staveley Lane

The Breck

76

3

Barrow Hill

Hill Grove

Oak Street

Brooks Road

Hall Lane

9

Campbell

Traffic Terrace

Road

Southgate Way

Chigwell Way

Drive

PO

Surgery

Barrow Hill Primary School

Barrow Hill Railway Centre

Clocktower Business Centre

Station

4

Handwood Farm

Barrow Hill

Cavendish Pl

475

Works Road

Business Centre

Works

Works

River Rother

5

Chesterfield Canal

441

Road

railway Staff ocial & Sports Club

Station Road

Oak Street

Beech St

Hollingwood Crs

Birch Lane

PO

Crescent

Troughbrook Road

Laburnum

Drive

Llan

Fir

42

A

B Hollingwd

C

D

Sycam

Street

St Jo

CLOWNE

14

23

CLINTHILL LANE

E F G H

52 53

Bondhay
Golf & Country Club

B6043

Cemetery

Highwood Lane

Way

Archaeological

Highwood

**Bakestone
Moor**

Archaeological Way

Hollin
Hill

Highwood Lane

Peter More Hill

HIGH STREET

Scotland Street

Greenway

High St

Portland Street

Hillside
Close

Hillside

Claylands Gv

Claylands Rd

Plantation
Cl

St Lawrence
View

Jubilee
Gdns

Jubilee Rd

Mason Street

Butt Hill

Butt Hill Cl

South
View

East Parade

Moor

Southfield Cl

Franklin Av

Franklin

Thorpe
Avenue

Sandy La

Longhurst

Southfield

Claylands Pl

Bakestone

New St

Sandy
Cl

Claylands Crs

Southfield
Industrial
Este

WORKSOP

Sunnyside

Longcroft
View

Whitwell
Sq

Health Cen

Malthouse
Rd

PO

Holmefi
Rd

Hangar Hill

Mill

Fox

Croft

Station

The
Poplar

Hennymoor Cl

Penny
Green

Middlegate

475

Longcroft
View

Mill

D

2

3

4

5

ROAD

Road

Hazelmere

Hazelmere
Farm

Markland
View

Hawthorne Av

Nobel
Cl

Chestnut
Dr

Haldane
Cl

Sycamore Cl

Maple
Dr

Orchard

Linden Rd

Rowan Cl

Skinner

Linden Dr

Baker St

Creswell Station

Creswell
Jun
Schoo

Gypsy
La

Douglas La

King St

Kings St

Queen St

PO

Ellen
Close

Creswell

Creswell
Leisure Centre

MANS

52 53

E F G H

Hartin
Drive

Devo

Beele
Close

Dri

Shakespeare Avenue

Tennyson Rd

West St

Eyre Street

Avenue

Street

Ann

Elmton Road

Welb

Church

Duke

Labur

Close

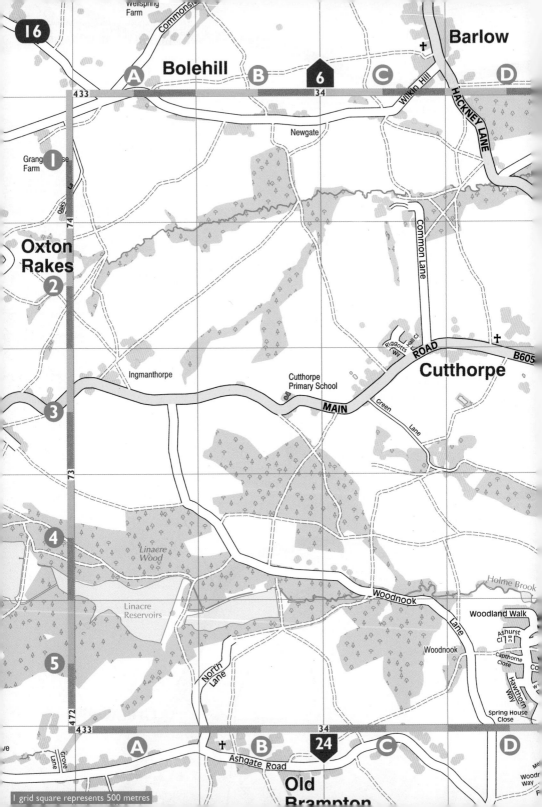

16

Bolehill

Ⓐ   Ⓑ   **6**   Ⓒ   Ⓓ

Barlow

Wellspring Farm

Commonside

433

34

Wilkin Hill

HACKNEY LANE

Newgate

Grange House Farm

1

Oaks La

74

Oxton Rakes

2

Common Lane

ROAD

Riggotts Wy

Hall Cl

Cutthorpe

B605

3

Ingmanthorpe

73

Cutthorpe Primary School

MAIN

Green Lane

4

Linacre Wood

Holme Brook

Woodnook Lane

Woodland Walk

Linacre Reservoirs

Ashurst Cl

Capthorne Close

Woodnook

5

472

North Lane

Hawthorn Way

Spring House Close

433

34

24

Ⓐ   Ⓑ   Ⓒ   Ⓓ

Grove Lane

Ashgate Road

Old Brampton

I grid square represents 500 metres

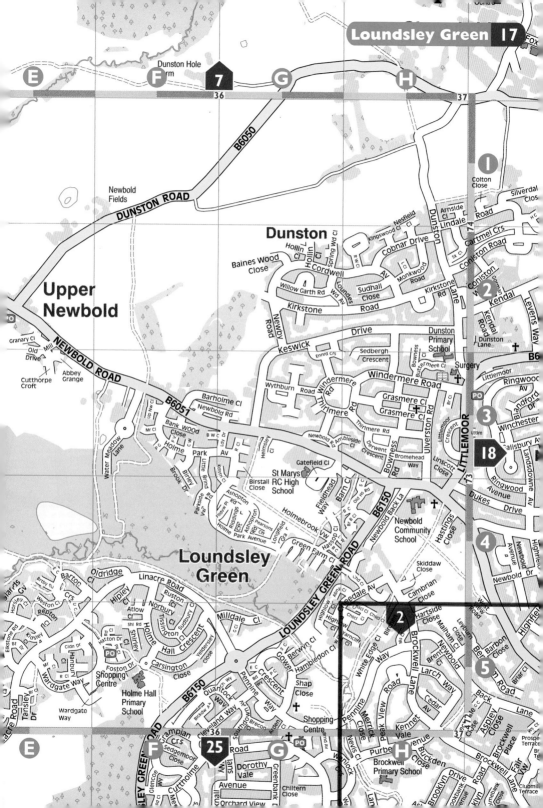

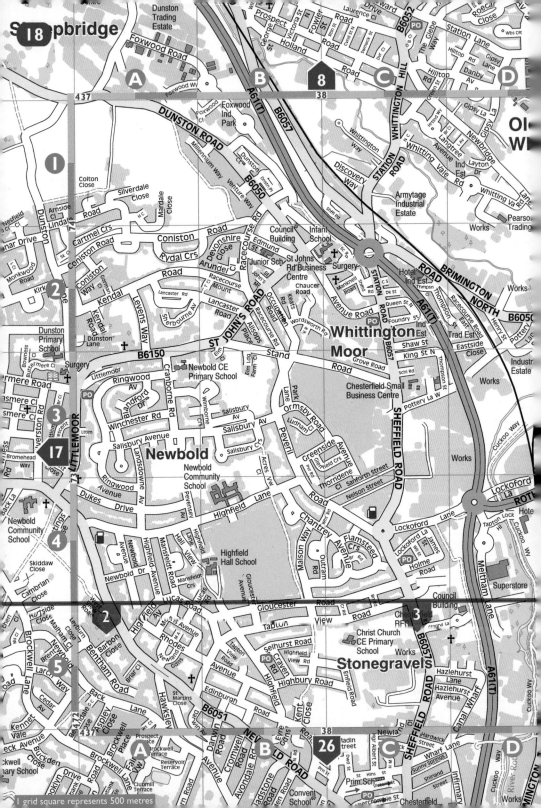

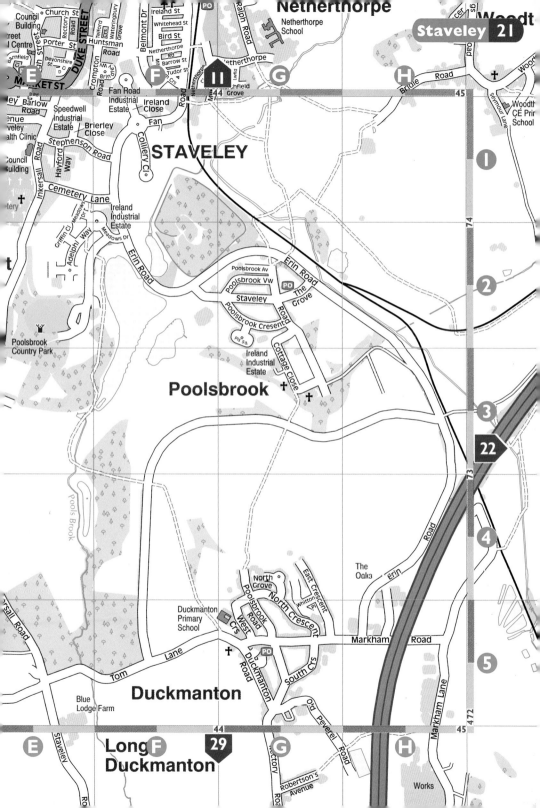

Netherthorpe

Woodt

STAVELEY

Poolsbrook

Poolsbrook
Country Park

Pools Brook

Duckmanton

Blue
Lodge Farm

**Long
Duckmanton**

Council
Building
Street
l Centre

Church St
Rectory
Road
Huntsman
Road

Belmont Dr
Whitehead St
Bird St

Ralph
Road

Netherthorpe
School

Porter St
Devonshire
St
Crompton
Road
Barrow St
Tudor St
Netherthorpe
Road

Netherthorpe

E

DUKE STREET

F

Netherthorpe
Road

144
H

hfield
Grove

G

Bridle Road

45

H

Woodthorpe
CE Prir
School

MARKET ST

Barlow
Road
Speedwell
Industrial
Estate
Brierley
Close

Fan Road
Industrial
Estate
Ireland
Close

eley
lth Clinic

Fan

Hayford
Way
Stephenson Road

Inkersall Road

Collery Cl

Council
Building

Cemetery Lane

Griffin Cl

Meadows Dr
Adelphi Way
Meadows Dr

Ireland
Industrial
Estate

Erin Road

74

I

Poolsbrook Av
Poolsbrook Vw
Staveley

PO

Erin Road

The
Grove

2

Poolsbrook Cresent

pl° sq.

Ireland
Industrial
Estate

Cottage Close

Road

3

22

73

Erin Road

4

The
Oaks

North
Grove

East Crescent
Whitton Pl

Poolsbrook Road

Duckmanton
Primary
School

North Crescent

West Crs

Markham Road

5

472

Staveley Road
Tom Lane

PO

South Crs

Old Peverel Road

Markham Lane

Duckmanton Road

45

44

E

Staveley Road

F

29

G

Robertson's
Avenue

H

Works

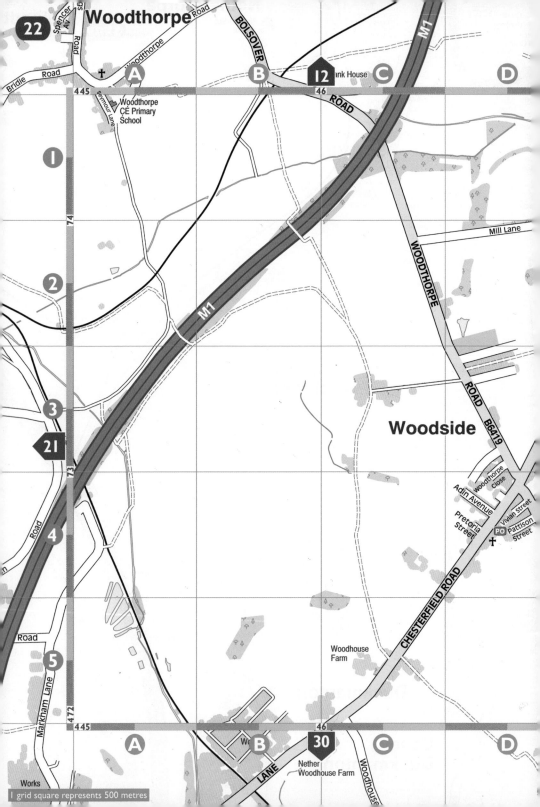

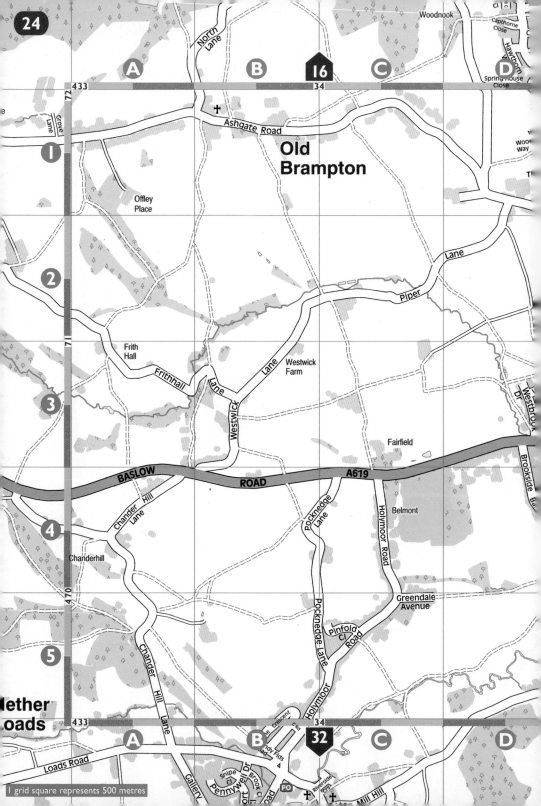

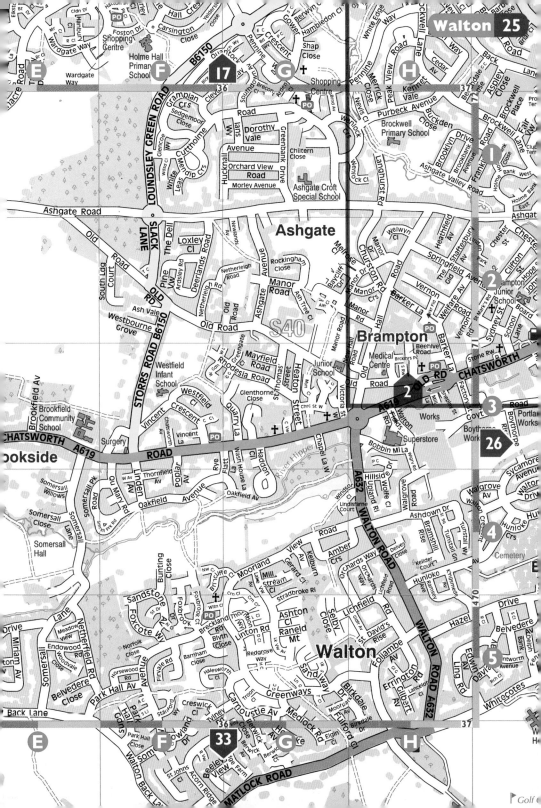

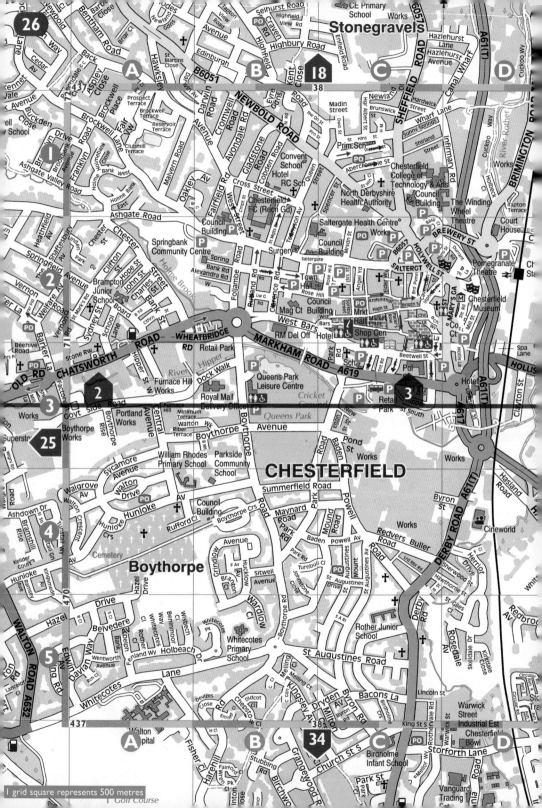

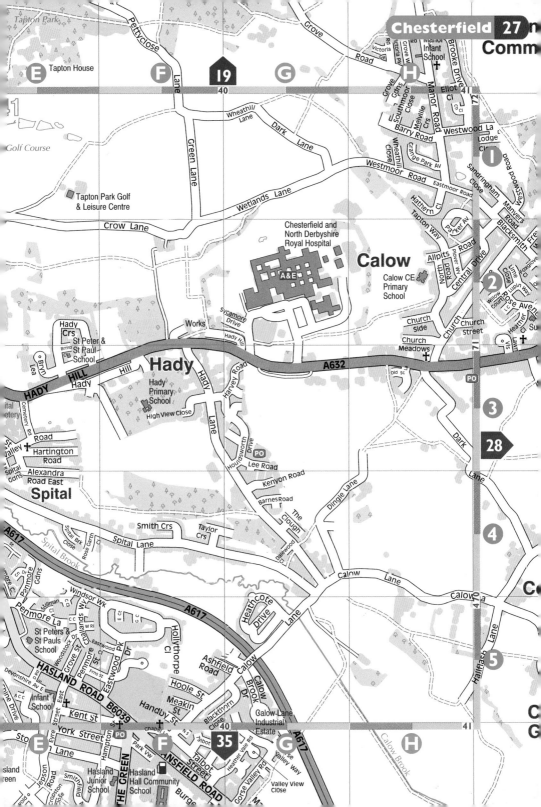

Brimington Common

28

20

Brooke Drive
Manor Infant School
Manor Road
Eliot Cl
Melville Crs
Grange Park Av
Westwood La
Lodge Close
Road
Eastmoor Road
Sandringham Close
Westwood Road
Hathern Cl
Tapton Way
Manvers Road
Parker Av
Freydon Wy
Brandene Cl
Blacksmith Lane
Allpits Road
Central Drive
Plover Wy
Lupin Wy
Foxglove Close
Willow Close
Lime Close
Orchid Close
Almond Close
Grace Avenue
Heather
Church Side
Church Street
Church Meadows
PO
Surgery
TOP ROAD
Oaks Farm Lane
Eastwood Drive
Nook Lane
Works Lane
CHESTERFIELD ROAD

Arkwright Town

Works Farm
Arkwright Primary School
Oak Tree Cl
Lime Tree Cl
School Lane
PO
Laurel Avenue
Rosling Way
A632
27
Lane

4

Bolehill

Cock Alley

Calow La
HallFlash Lane
Back Lane
DEEPSICK LANE
B6425
MOOR LANE
B6425

5

Calow Green

36

West Brook Farm

1 grid square represents 500 metres

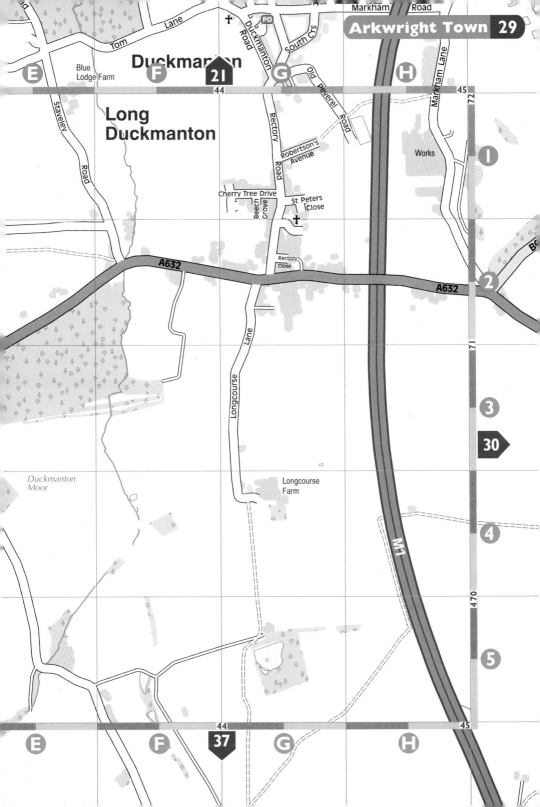

Elmton Park

E F **23** G H

48 49 72

Featherbed Road

ROAD

B6419

Lodge Farm

Cemetery

Oxcroft Lane

Mill Walk

Mill Lane

Quarry Road

Limekiln Field

Oxcroft Lane

Bank Close

Wro Cl

New Cl

St

Police Sta

Stratton Road

Limekiln Fields Road

Farnsworth Farm

I

2

Bolsov Moor

ROTHERHAM ROAD

B6417

HILL TOP

Hides Gn

Gardeners Ct

Dykes Cl

Steel Lane

Elmton Lane

Maripit Lane

Bolsover Local Hospital

3

BOLSOVER

A632

le Street
cal Cen

Longlands Road

Welbeck Road

Council Building

Bolsover Infant School

Bolsover Clinic

Horsehead Lane

Cornmill Close

Cedar Park Drive

Beck Close

Meadowlands

Bretton Av

Sycamore Close

P

P

Castle
street

O-Del Off
Fire Sta

P

P

PO

St
Church

rth Derbyshire
tiary College

TOWN END

HORNSCROFT Road

The Paddock

Orchard Cl

Ridgeway Av

Cherry Tree Cl

Sandhills

Holbeck Rd

Lilac Grove

Stables Court

Elm Close

Langstone Avenue

4

LANGWITH ROAD

Cotton St

High St

Moor Lane

Smithson Avenue

Portland Avenue

Huntingdon Avenue

Laburnum Cl

Langstone Avenue

station

Lords Cl

Ridgedale Rd

Highfield Road

Sears Ct

Spittal Rd

Brookfield Rd

Avondale Rd

Portland Crs

Moorfield Sq

Moorfield Avenue

470

ay

ley

Ridgedale Road

Fairfield Rd

Conduit Rd

Cromwell Rd

Cavendish Rd

Scarsdale Crescent

Portland Avenue

Cavendish Road

St Lawrence Avenue

Eastern Av

Stockley View

Tower Crs

Cavendish Rd

A632

5 LANGWI

Owlcotes View

Crich View

Darwood

Sutton View

West View

Castle Green

Huds on Mt

Victoria St

Nesbit St

Cross St

Middle St

Wells St

Selwyn Street

PO

Hills Town

48 49

E F G H

nt Av

P

ansfield Road

Hillstown Business Centre

ROTHERHAM ROAD

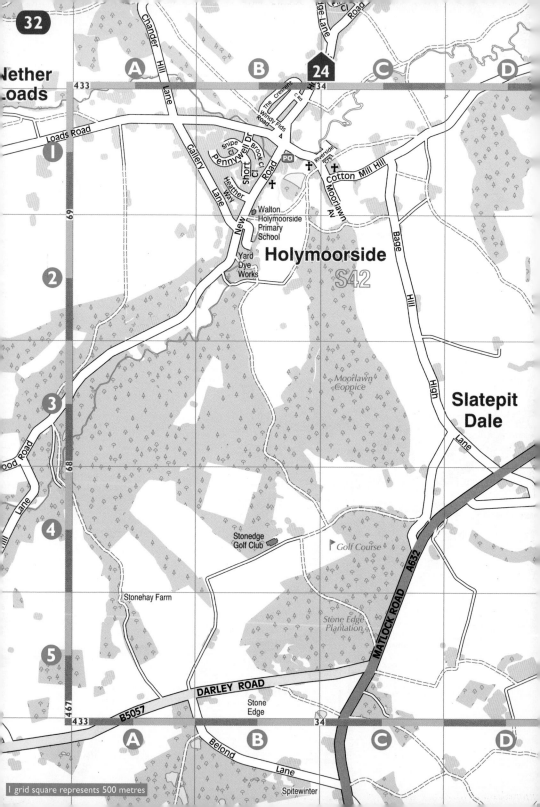

Nether Loads

A　　　B　　　**24**　　　C　　　D

Changer Hill Lane

Loads Road

The Crescent

Windy Flats Road

Cr Rd

Ht

34

1

433

69

Gallery Lane

Heather Way

New St

Short Cl

Pennywell Dr

snipe

Brook Cl

Road

PO

Riverside Cres

Cotton Mill Hill

Moorlawn Av

Walton Holymoorside Primary School

2

Yard Dye Works

Holymoorside
S42

Bage Hill

3

68

Moorlawn Coppice

High Lane

Slatepit Dale

ood Road

Lane

4

Stonedge Golf Club

Golf Course

A632

MATLOCK ROAD

Stonehay Farm

Stone Edge Plantation

5

467

433

B5057

DARLEY ROAD

Stone Edge

34

A　　　B　　　C　　　D

Belond Lane

Spitewinter

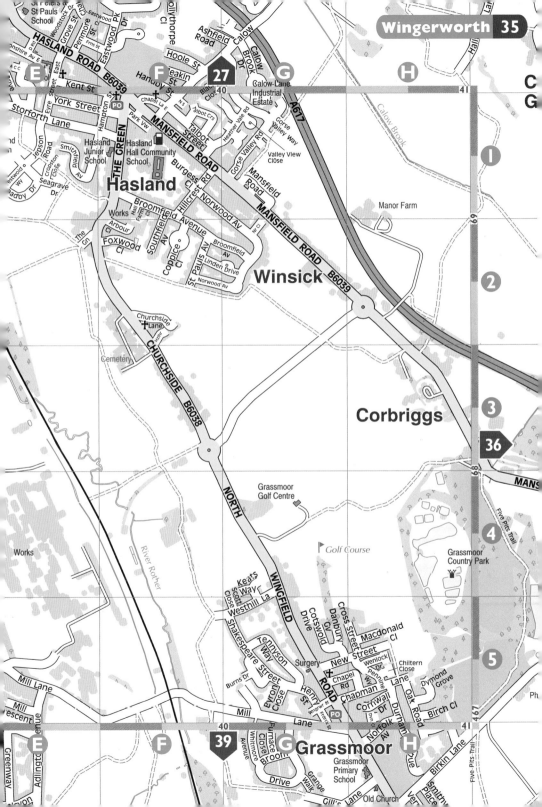

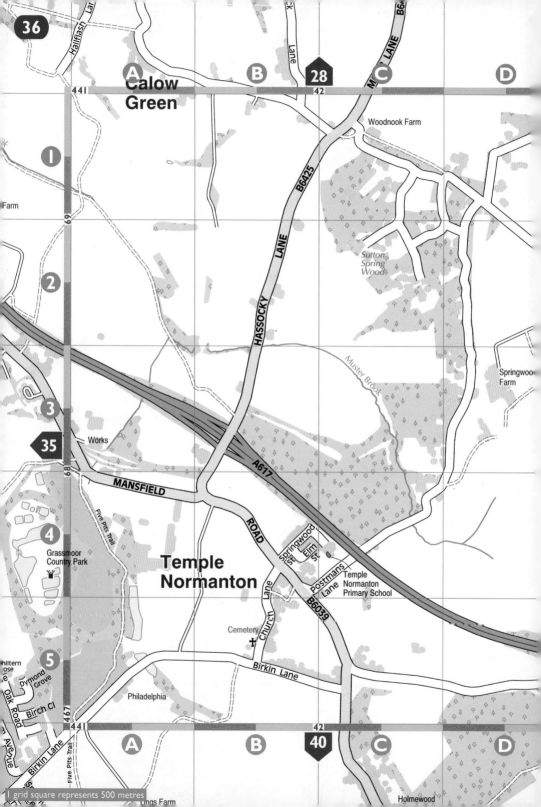

E F **29** G H

I

M1

69

2

Sutton Lane

Sutton
Scarsdale Hall

Works

Rock Lane

**Sutton
Scarsdale**

Palterton Lane

Works

Mill Hill

3

69

Owlcotes

4

Shire Lane

High House
Farm

A617

5

Mansfield Road

Heath
Common

Church Lane

E F **4I** G H

Vicarage
Close

Five Pits Trail

Slack

Drive

Lilac
Close

Heath PO

Wilson Lane

Mill Lane

Ph

E

F

35 40 Mill

G

H

41

67

Five Pits Trail

I

Adlington Avenue

Mill Crescent

Halcyon

Shakespeare Street

Tennyson Way

Burns Dr

Surgery

New Street

Henry St

Wingfield St

Chapel Rd

Chapman St

Wenlock Dr

Pennine

Chiltern Close

Dymond Grove

ROAD

Cornwall

Norfolk AV

Durham Avenue

Birch Cl

Furnace Close

Whitmore Avenue

Broom Drive

Grange Walk

Gill's Lane

Old Church School

Birkin La W

Birkin Lane

Smithy Place

Vernon Rd

Southend

Grassmoor

Grassmoor Primary School

B6038

2

CHESTERFIELD ROAD

Bridgewater Street

Dale Crs

Dale Rd

Queen

Birkin AV

North Side Surgery

Victoria Road

Bridge St

Tupton Primary School

PO

Green La

Ivanhoe

Wy Mt

Ward Street

Ankerbold Road

Rother Cft

Farm View

Pond La

Ankerbold Road

Deincourt Crescent

Alma

Evam Cl

3

Deincourt Community School

40

Elvin Way

Madin St

Wingfield Road

Davenport Road

Statham AV

Sales AV

Ford Street

Hoades St

Jackson Av

Ankerbold Farm

Longcroft Close

Tupton

Redfern St

North Wingfield Junior School

North Wingfield Infant School

The Medical Centre

Wayside Cl

Ashford

Calver AV

White Lea Avenue

Nethermoor Road

Park Road

Brassington

Station New Road

Hepthorne Lane

Midland View

Park View

Blacks

Torrani Wy

Draycott Road

Bright St

Crich Place

4

il Building

PO

Williac Clo

A6175 465

NORT WING

Tupton Hall School

Occupation La

Alma St

PO

Berry Street

Knighton Street

John Street

George St

North St

Station Road

Cross St

New Street

Leigh Way

Hambleton AV

Mayfield Drive

Jham Cl

Bamford Av

Lincoln Way

Winchester Close

Fairfield Drive

Little

5

St LAWRENCE ROAD

Glebe Gdns

Elvaston

Parwich Road

Church Tree La

Longhaw Cl

Edensor Close

Cherry Tree GV

Severn Crs

Morton Road

Elton Close

Tansley Road

Church Meadows Rd

Wensley Rd

church Paddock

E

F

43

G

H

40

41

Church

40

36

Birkin Lane

Chilte Close
Dymond Grove
Oak Road
Birch Cl
Birkin Lane

A
adelphia

B

C

D

Smithy Place
Vernon Ri
Southend

1

441
67

Lings Farm

Holmewood Business Park

Williamthorpe Industrial Park

Tupton Way

Mo Clo

Enterprise Drive

CHESTERFIELD

B6038

2

B6039

ROAD

Park Road

H

Five Pits Trail

Shelley Street
Tennyson
Shakespeare
Shaw St
Avenu
Lvenu

Deincourt Crescent

CHESTERFIELD

99

Alma Road

Evam Cl

Hucklow Av

Lings Crs

Haddon Road

Curbar Cl

Five Pits Trail

Williamthorpe

Masefield

Searston Avenue

Glebe Cl

Chu

Cable Close

3

Deincourt

39

North Wingfield Junior School

North Wingfield Infant School

Alice's View

The Medical Centre
Wayside Cl

Calver Av

Ashford Cl

White Leas Avenue

Highfields

Williamthorpe Rd

Highfields Dr

Meadow View

Williamthorpe Rd

PO

ROAD

ROAD

rani Wy

4

Draycott Road

Bright St

Council Building

PO

WILLIAMTHORPE

Williamthorpe Close

Dark Lane

Holbrook Av

Ayincourt Rd

Cressbrook Av

Elyn Avenue

Five Pits Trail

A61 A65

Crich Place

Cromford Close

NORTH WINGFIELD

NCE ROAD

5

Edensor Close

Longdrav

arwich Road

Little

Morton Road

Fairfield Drive

uston Road
Cherry Tree Cv
Church Ley
Meadows

Severn Crs

Tansley Road

Eiton Close

A

B

C

D

Seanor Farm

1 grid square represents 500 metres

Mansfield Road

E F **37** G H +

Church Lane

Heath Common

Vicarage Close

Heath PO

Wilson Lane

I

Five Pits Trail

Moorland Drive

Lilac Close

Gorse Bank

Slack Lane

Main Road

Mill La

Mill Lane

2

Heather Av

Bracken Av

Brmb Cl

Heath Primary School

Fern Cl

A6175

Chapel Hill

Park Road

Road

od

Wood St

Dukes Close

Cavendish Cl

Cl

Orsley

Heath Road

Compton St

Hardwickst Albans

Hunoke Rd

Cl

HEATH ROAD

PO + Cl

entre

Old Colliery Lane

Barnfield Close

Five Pits Trail

al

Astwith Close

Stainsby Close

Hardwick View Road

Holmewood Industrial Estate

3

Stainsby

4

B6039

Hawking Lane

Out Lane

465

Stainsby Common

Common End

Stainsby Pond

5

E F G H

Lane

Branch Lane

Astwith Lane

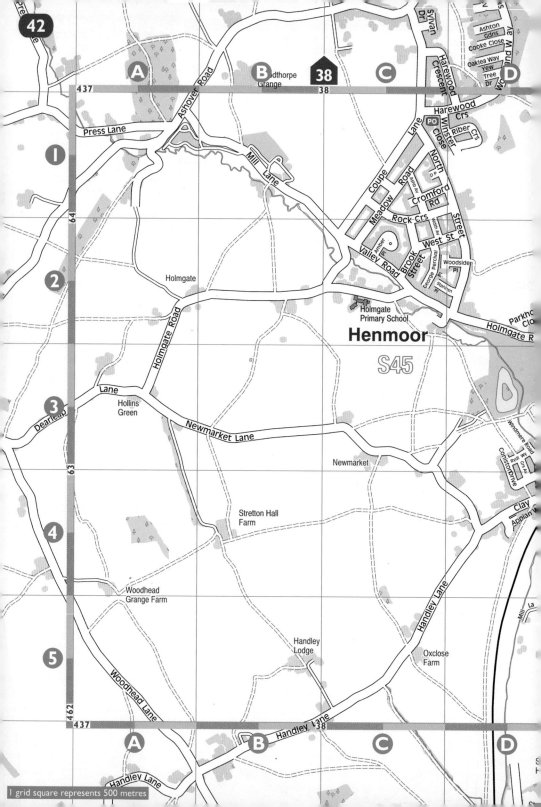

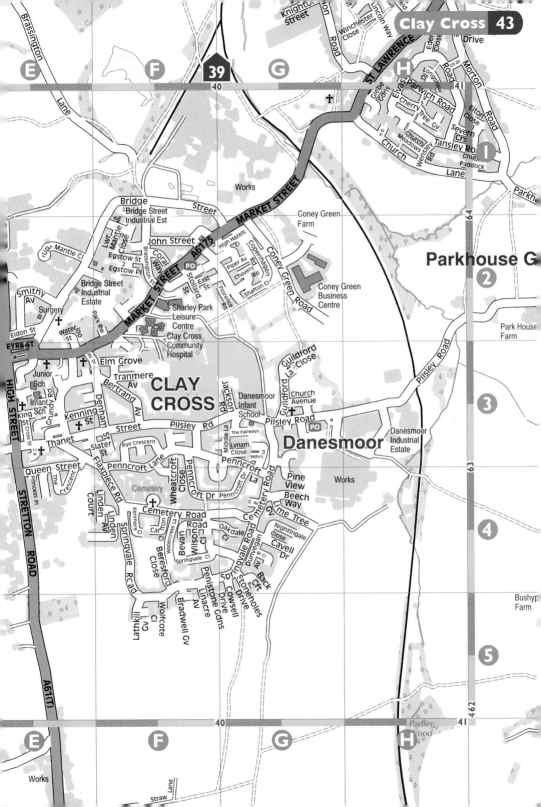

E F 39 G H

40

41

Brassington Lane

Knighton Street

Winchester Close

Lincoln Way

Drive

 St Lawrence Road

Ch Dr

Eder Close

Morton Road

Glebe Gdns

Elvas Close

Parwich Road

Elton Road

Cherry Tree Gv

Severn Crs

Tansley Rd

Longmead Cl

Church Cl

Church Meadows

Wensly Rd

H D

Church Lane

Church Paddock

Parkh

I

64

Works

Street

Market Street

Bridge Street

Bridge Street Industrial Est

Coney Green Farm

Parkhouse G

2

Park House Farm

John Street

A617s

High Hazels

Piper Av

Copenhagen

Coney Green Road

Lwr Mantle Close

Upr Mantle Cl

Coral Way

Egstow St

Egstow Pl

Brassington St

Market Street

PO

Stollard St

East St

East St

Florence Rd

Chavern Rd

Shafton Cl

Coney Green Business Centre

Smithy Av

Surgery

Bridge Street Industrial Estate

Park RW

Eldon St

Water St

Br Cl

Sharley Park Leisure Centre

Clay Cross Community Hospital

Guildford La

Guildford Close

Pilsley Road

EYRE ST

Elm Grove

CLAY CROSS

Jackson Rd

Danesmoor Infant School

Church Avenue

Guildford Rd

3

63

Junior Sch

Tranmere Av

Bertrand Av

Denham Av

Pilsley Rd

Pilsley Road

PO

Danesmoor

Danesmoor Industrial Estate

High Street

Infant Sch

Kenning St

Grundy Rd

King St

Street

The Fairways

Middle

Lynam Close

Nthr C

Danesmoor

Thanet

St Cross St

Slater St

Rye Crescent

Penncroft Lane

Wheatcroft Close

Penncroft Dr

Penncroft

Penncroft La

Penncroft Cl

Pine View

Beech Way

Works

4

Queen Street

The Crescent

Princess Pl

Flaxpiece Rd

Cemetery

Linden Court

Linden Av

Springvale Road

Kenmere Cl

Cemetery Road

Watercross La

Carlton

Bevan Road

Springvale Cl

Oakdale Cl

Dunvegan

Cemetery Road

G Av

Back

Lime Tree

Nightingale Close

Cavell Dr

Bushyp Farm

STRETTON ROAD

A61(T)

Beresford Close

Lathkill Gv

Wolfcote Cl

Bradwell Gv

Penistone Gdns

Linacre

Springvale Drive

Cowsell Drive

Stoneholes Crt

Nicholls

5

462

Padley Wood

E F G H

40

41

Works

Straw Lane

Arkwright Town 28 C3	Corbriggs 35 H3	Holmewood 40 D2	Slatepit Dale ....
Ashgate 25 G2	Cowley 4 B5	Holymoorside 32 B2	Snape Hill ....
Bakestone Moor 15 F2	Creswell 15 H5	Inkersall Green 20 D4	Spital ....
Barlow 6 D5	Crowhole 6 B3	Limekiln Field 31 F2	Stainsby ....
Barrow Hill 10 A3	Cutthorpe 16 C3	Long Duckmanton 29 F1	Stanfree ....
Birdholme 34 B1	Danesmoor 43 G3	Loundsley Green 17 F4	Staveley ....
Bolehill 6 A5	Dronfield 5 G3	Mastin Moor 12 B3	Stonegravels ....
Bolehill 28 B4	Duckmanton 21 F5	Middlecroft 20 D2	Stubbley ....
Bolsover 31 E3	Dunston 17 G2	Nether Handley 9 H1	Sutton Scarsdale ....
Boythorpe 26 A4	Gosforth Valley 4 B2	Nether Moor 38 C2	Swathwick ....
Brampton 2 A6	Grassmoor 39 G1	Netherthorpe 11 G5	Tapton ....
Brimington 19 H3	Hady 27 F3	Newbold 18 A3	Temple Normanton ....
Brimington Common 20 A5	Hallowes 5 G4	New Bolsover 30 B3	Tupton ....
Brindwoodgate 6 A2	Harlesthorpe 14 A2	New Brimington 19 G1	Unstone Green ....
Brookside 25 E3	Hasland 35 F1	New Whittington 9 E3	Upper Newbold ....
The Brushes 8 B3	Heath 41 G1	North Wingfield 40 A5	Walton ....
Calow 27 H2	Henmoor 42 C2	Old Brampton 24 B1	Whittington Moor ....
Calow Green 28 A5	Hepthorne Lane 39 G4	Old Tupton 38 D4	Williamthorpe ....
Carr Vale 30 D5	Highfields 40 B3	Old Whittington 18 D1	Wingerworth ....
Clay Cross 43 F3	Hills Town 31 G5	Oxcroft Estate 23 G3	Winsick ....
Clowne 13 H3	Hockley 38 C1	Parkhouse Green 43 H2	Woodside ....
Cock Alley 28 A4	Hill Top 5 E5	Poolsbrook 21 F3	Woodthorpe ....
Common End 41 F5	Hollingwood 20 B1	Sheepbridge 7 H5	
Common Side 6 B4	Holmesdale 5 G2	Shuttlewood 23 E4	

USING THE STREET INDEX

Street names are listed alphabetically. Each street name is followed by its postal town or area locality, the Postcode District, the page number, and the reference to the square in which the name is found.

Standard index entries are shown as follows:

Abbey Gra *RCH* S42 ....**17** E3

Street names and selected addresses not shown on the map due to scale restrictions are shown in the index with an asterisk or with the name of an adjoining road in brackets:

Amesbury CI *CHNE* * S41...............**18** A3

Almond PI
STV/CWN
(off Chesterfield Rd) S43 ....**19** G3

GENERAL ABBREVIATIONS

ACC....................ACCESS	DRO.......................DROVE	JCT....................JUNCTION	PROM....................PROME
ALY.......................ALLEY	DRY...................DRIVEWAY	JTY.........................JETTY	PRS....................PRI
AP...................APPROACH	DWGS...............DWELLINGS	KG...........................KING	PRT.......................
AR.......................ARCADE	E..............................EAST	KNL.......................KNOLL	PT...........................
ASS...............ASSOCIATION	EMB.............EMBANKMENT	L..............................LAKE	PTH........................
AV.......................AVENUE	EMBY...................EMBASSY	LA...........................LANE	PZ...........................F
BCH.......................BEACH	ESP.................ESPLANADE	LDG.......................LODGE	QD.......................QUAD
BLDS.................BUILDINGS	EST.........................ESTATE	LGT.........................LIGHT	QU...........................Q
BND........................BEND	EX...................EXCHANGE	LK...........................LOCK	QY...........................
BNK........................BANK	EXPY...............EXPRESSWAY	LKS.........................LAKES	R.............................
BR.......................BRIDGE	EXT..................EXTENSION	LNDG.................LANDING	RBT....................ROUNDA
BRK.......................BROOK	F/O...................FLYOVER	LTL.........................LITTLE	RD...........................
BTM.....................BOTTOM	FC.............FOOTBALL CLUB	LWR.......................LOWER	RDG.......................F
BUS..................BUSINESS	FK...........................FORK	MAG.............MAGISTRATE	REP.......................REP
BVD.................BOULEVARD	FLD.........................FIELD	MAN..................MANSIONS	RES.......................RESER
BY.......................BYPASS	FLDS.......................FIELDS	MD...........................MEAD	RFC.........RUGBY FOOTBALL
CATH................CATHEDRAL	FLS.........................FALLS	MDW...................MEADOWS	RI...........................
CEM..................CEMETERY	FLS.........................FLATS	MEM..................MEMORIAL	RP............................F
CEN.......................CENTRE	FM...........................FARM	MKT.......................MARKET	RW...........................
CFT.........................CROFT	FT.............................FORT	MKTS...................MARKETS	S............................S
CH.......................CHURCH	FWY....................FREEWAY	ML............................MALL	SCH......................SC
CHA.......................CHASE	FY.........................FERRY	ML............................MILL	SE.......................SOUTH
CHYD...............CHURCHYARD	GA...........................GATE	MNR.......................MANOR	SER...................SERVICE
CIR.........................CIRCLE	GAL.....................GALLERY	MS...........................MEWS	SH...........................
CIRC...................CIRCUS	GDN....................GARDEN	MSN..................MISSION	SHOP....................SHOP
CL...........................CLOSE	GDNS...................GARDENS	MT...........................MOUNT	SKWY......................SKY
CLFS.......................CLIFFS	GLD.........................GLADE	MTN................MOUNTAIN	SMT......................SU
CMP.........................CAMP	GLN...........................GLEN	MTS..............MOUNTAINS	SOC......................SOC
CNR.......................CORNER	GN...........................GREEN	MUS..................MUSEUM	SP............................
CO.........................COUNTY	GND.......................GROUND	MWY................MOTORWAY	SPR.......................SP
COLL...................COLLEGE	GRA.......................GRANGE	N...........................NORTH	SQ........................SQU
COM.....................COMMON	GRG.......................GARAGE	NE..................NORTH EAST	ST...........................ST
COMM.............COMMISSION	GT...........................GREAT	NW.................NORTH WEST	STN.......................STA
CON..................CONVENT	GTWY...................GATEWAY	O/P...................OVERPASS	STR.......................STR
COT.....................COTTAGE	GV...........................GROVE	OFF.........................OFFICE	STRD.....................STR
COTS.................COTTAGES	HGR.......................HIGHER	ORCH................ORCHARD	SW...............SOUTH W
CP...........................CAPE	HL...........................HILL	OV...........................OVAL	TDG.....................TRAI
CPS.......................COPSE	HLS.........................HILLS	PAL.........................PALACE	TER.......................TER
CR...........................CREEK	HO.........................HOUSE	PAS....................PASSAGE	THWY...............THROUGH
CREM..............CREMATORIUM	HOL.......................HOLLOW	PAV..................PAVILION	TNL.......................TUN
CRS...................CRESCENT	HOSP..................HOSPITAL	PDE.........................PARADE	TOLL.......................TOLL
CSWY...................CAUSEWAY	HRB.......................HARBOUR	PH..............PUBLIC HOUSE	TPK.......................TURN
CT...........................COURT	HTH.........................HEATH	PK...........................PARK	TR.........................TR
CTRL...................CENTRAL	HTS.......................HEIGHTS	PKWY...................PARKWAY	TRL...........................T
CTS.......................COURTS	HVN.......................HAVEN	PL...........................PLACE	TWR.......................TO
CTYD...................COURTYARD	HWY.......................HIGHWAY	PLN.........................PLAIN	U/P..................UNDER
CUTT...................CUTTINGS	IMP.....................IMPERIAL	PLNS.......................PLAINS	UNI...................UNIVER
CV...........................COVE	IN.............................INLET	PLZ.......................PLAZA	UPR........................UP
CYN.......................CANYON	IND EST........INDUSTRIAL ESTATE	POL............POLICE STATION	V.............................
DEPT................DEPARTMENT	INF....................INFIRMARY	PR.........................PRINCE	VA.........................VA
DL...........................DALE	INFO................INFORMATION	PREC................PRECINCT	VIAD....................VIAD
DM...........................DAM	INT.................INTERCHANGE	PREP..............PREPARATORY	VIL...........................V
DR...........................DRIVE	IS...........................ISLAND	PRIM...................PRIMARY	VIS...........................

.....VILLAGE	W ....WEST	WK ....WALK	WY ....WAY
.....VILLAS	WD ....WOOD	WKS ....WALKS	YD ....YARD
.....VIEW	WHF ....WHARF	WLS ....WELLS	YHA...............................YOUTH HOSTEL

TCODE TOWNS AND AREA ABBREVIATIONS

.....Bolsover	CLCR.....Clay Cross	RCH .....Rural Chesterfield	WRKS.....Worksop south
.....Chesterfield north & east	DRON.....Dronfield	SBK/MW .....Shirebrook/Market Warsop	
.....Chesterfield south & west	ECK/KIL.....Eckington/Killamarsh	STV/CWN.....Staveley/Clowne	

dex - streets

Abb - Bro

A

Aspley Cl *CHSW* S40 ....2 C3
Aston Cl *DRON* S18..............5 G1
Astwith Cl *BSVR* S44 ....41 F2
Athol Cl *CHSW* S40..............25 F5
Atlow Cl *CHSW* S40..............17 F5
Attlee Rd *STV/CWN* S45..............20 B3
Avenue 1 *CHNE* S41 ....26 D5
Avenue 2 *CHNE* S41 ....26 D5
Avenue 3 *CHNE* S41 ....26 D5
Avenue 4 *CHNE* S41 ....26 D5
Avenue 5 *CHNE* S41 ....26 D5
Avenue 6 *CHNE* * S41 ....26 D5
Avenue 7 *CHNE* S41 ....26 D5
Avenue 8 *CHNE* S41 ....26 D5
Avenue Rd *CHNE* S41 ....18 C2
The Avenue *DRON* S18..............5 F2
Aviemore Cl *STV/CWN* S43 ....9 G3
Avon Cl *DRON* S18..............5 F1
Avondale Rd *BSVR* S44 ....31 E5
  CHSW S40 ....2 E4
  STV/CWN S43 ....20 C3
Ayncourt Rd *RCH* S42 ....40 B4

B

Back Cft *CLCR* S45 ....43 G4
Back La *BSVR* S44 ....28 B5
  STV/CWN (off Mitchell St) S43 ......14 B3
Back South St *STV/CWN* S43 ......9 F4
Bacons La *CHSW* S40 ....26 C5
Baden Powell Av *CHSW* S40 ......26 B4
Baden Powell Rd *CHSW* S40 ......26 C3
Bage Hl *RCH* S42 ....32 C2
Bainbridge Rd *BSVR* S44 ....30 D4
Baines Wood Cl *CHNE* S41 ......17 G2
Baker St *WRKS* S80..............15 G5
Bakestone Moor *WRKS* S80 ......15 G2
Bakewell Rd *STV/CWN* S43 ......20 C5
Ballidon Cl *CHSW* S40 ....17 G4
Balmoak La *CHNE* S41 ....19 E5
Balmoral Crs *DRON* S18..............4 B5
Balmoral Wy *STV/CWN* S43 ....9 G3
Bamford Av *RCH* S42 ....39 H4
Bamford Rd *STV/CWN* S43 ......20 C4
Bamford St *STV/CWN* S43 ....9 F3
Bank Cl *BSVR* S44 ....31 E2
Bank Rd *CHNE* S41 ....18 C4
Bank St *CHSW* S40 ....2 D6
  STV/CWN S43 ....9 F2
Bank Wood Cl *CHSW* S40 ......17 F5
Barbon Cl *CHSW* S40 ....2 C1
Bar Cft *CHSW* S40 ....17 H4
Barholme Cl *CHNE* S41 ....17 F3
Barker Fold *CHSW* S40 ....2 B6
Barker La *CHSW* S40 ....2 A6
Barlborough Rd *STV/CWN* S43......13 H2
Barley La *CHSW* S40 ....17 E5
Barlow Lees La *DRON* S18..............4 D5
Barlow Rd *CHNE* S41 ....16 D1
  STV/CWN S43 ....11 E5
Barlow Vw *DRON* S18..............5 E5
Barnard Av *DRON* S18..............5 H1
Barn Cl *CHSW* S40 ....17 G4
Barnes Av *DRON* S18..............4 B2
Barnes La *DRON* S18..............4 B1
Barnes Rd *CHNE* S41 ....27 G4
Barnfield Cl *RCH* S42 ....41 E3
  STV/CWN S43 ....11 E5
Barnham Cl *CHSW* S40 ....25 F5
Barrow St *STV/CWN* S43 ....11 F5
Barry Rd *STV/CWN* S43 ....27 H1
Barton Crs *CHNE* S41 ....17 E4
Barton St *STV/CWN* S43 ....14 B3
Basil Cl *CHNE* S41 ....3 H5
Baslow Rd *RCH* S42 ....24 A4
Bateman Cl *STV/CWN* S43 ....9 F3
Bate Wood Av *STV/CWN* S43 ......20 B5
Bathurst Rd *BSVR* S44 ....30 C4
Baycliff Dr *CHSW* S40 ....2 B2
Beck Cl *BSVR* S44 ....31 G3
Beechdale Cl *CHSW* S40 ....2 B3

Beech Dr *BSVR* S44 ....28 D2
Beech Gv *BSVR* S44 ....29 G1
Beech St *STV/CWN* S43 ....20 A1
Beech Tree Dr *STV/CWN* S43 ......14 B5
Beech Wy *CLCR* S45 ....43 G4
  DRON * S18..............5 E1
Beechwood Rd *DRON* S18..............4 D3
Beehive Rd *CHSW* S40 ....2 A6
Beeley Cl *RCH* S42 ....40 A4
  STV/CWN S43 ....20 C4
Beeley Vw *CHSW* S40 ....33 F1
Beeston Cl *DRON* S18..............4 A2
Beetwell St *CHSW* S40 ....3 H7
Belfit Dr *RCH* S42 ....38 B1
Belle Vue Cl *STV/CWN* S43 ......19 F2
Bell House La *STV/CWN* S43 ......11 F4
Bellhouse Vw
  STV/CWN (off Bellhouse La) S43 ....11 F4
Belmont Dr *STV/CWN* S43 ......11 F5
Belton Cl *DRON* S18..............4 A3
Belvedere Av *CHSW* S40 ......26 A5
Belvedere Cl *RCH* S42 ......25 E5
Beninmoor Wy *CHSW* S40 ......26 A5
Bennison Gdns *CLCR* * S45 ......43 F3
Bentham Rd *CHSW* S40 ....2 C1
Bentinck Dr *STV/CWN* S43 ......14 C3
Bent La *STV/CWN* S43 ....11 G4
Bents Crs *DRON* S18..............5 G1
Bents La *DRON* S18..............5 G1
Beresford Cl *CLCR* S45 ......43 F4
Bernard Av *STV/CWN* S43 ......19 H1
Berry St *RCH* S42 ....39 G5
Bertrand Av *CLCR* S45 ......43 F3
Berwick Av *CHSW* S40 ......33 G1
Berwick Cl *CHSW* S40 ......25 G5
Berwick Ct *CHSW* S40 ......33 G1
Berwyn Cl *CHSW* S40 ......17 G5
Bestwood Dr *CLCR* S45 ......43 E3
Bevan Dr *STV/CWN* S43 ......20 B3
Bevan Rd *CLCR* S45 ....43 F4
Bilby La *STV/CWN* S43 ....19 G1
Birch Cl *RCH* S42 ....35 H5
Birchen Cl *CHSW* S40 ....2 A1
  DRON S18..............4 B3
Birch Holt Gv *DRON* S18..............8 A2
Birchitt Vw *DRON* S18..............5 E1
Birch Kiln Cft *STV/CWN* S43 ......19 H2
Birch La *STV/CWN* S43 ......20 A1
Birchwood Crs *CHSW* S40 ......34 B1
Birdholme Crs *CHSW* S40 ......26 C5
Bird St *STV/CWN* S43 ....11 F5
Birkdale Dr *CHSW* S40 ......25 G5
Birkin Av *RCH* S42 ....39 E2
Birkin La *RCH* S42 ....39 H1
Birkin La West *RCH* S42 ......39 H1
Birley Brook Dr *CHSW* S40 ......17 F3
Birstall Cl *CHSW* S40 ......17 G4
Blackdown Av *CHSW* S40 ......17 F5
Blacksmith La *STV/CWN* S43 ......28 A2
Blackthorn Cl *CHNE* S41 ......35 F1
Blandford Dr *CHNE* S41 ......18 A3
Blind La *BSVR* S44 ....30 D2
Bluebank Vw *CHNE* S41 ....9 F4
Blue Bell Cl *STV/CWN* S43 ......20 B5
Blueberry Cl *STV/CWN* S43 ......20 B5
Blue Lodge Cl *STV/CWN* S43 ......20 B5
Blunt Av *STV/CWN* S43 ......20 C5
Blyth Cl *CHSW* S40 ....25 F5
Bobbin Mill La *CHSW* S40 ......25 H3
Bodmin Wy *CHSW* S40 ......17 G5
Bolsover Rd *STV/CWN* S43 ......12 B5
Bondfield Rd *STV/CWN* S43 ......20 C3
Bond St *STV/CWN* S43 ....20 C2
Border Cl *STV/CWN* S43 ......14 B4
Border La *STV/CWN* S43 ......14 B4
Bottom Rd *RCH* S42 ....38 A1
Boughton La *STV/CWN* S43 ......13 H5
Boulton Cl *RCH* S42 ....17 E5
Boundary Cl *STV/CWN* S43 ......11 G4
Bourne Cl *STV/CWN* S43 ......19 G2
Bowdon Av *STV/CWN* S43 ......13 E1
Bowland Dr *CHSW* S40 ......33 F1
Bowness Cl *CHNE* S41 ......17 H3

  DRON S18..............4 C3
Bowness Rd *CHNE* S41 ......17 H3
Boythorpe Av *CHSW* S40 ......26 B3
Boythorpe Crs *CHSW* S40 ......26 B4
Boythorpe Mt *CHSW* S40 ......26 B3
Boythorpe Ri *CHSW* S40 ......26 A3
Boythorpe Rd *CHSW* S40 ......2 E7
Bracken Av *BSVR* S44 ......41 F2
Brackendale Cl *CLCR* S45 ......43 G4
  STV/CWN S43 ......19 F3
Brackens La *STV/CWN* S43 ......13 F1
Bradbourne Cl *STV/CWN* S43 ......20 C2
Bradbury Cl
  CHSW
  (off School Board La) S40 ......2 C6
Bradbury Dr *RCH* S42 ......33 H4
Bradley Wy *STV/CWN* S43 ......19 G3
Bradshaw Rd *STV/CWN* S43 ......20 B4
Bradwell Cl *DRON* S18..............4 A3
Bradwell Gv *CLCR* S45 ......43 F5
Bradwell Pl *STV/CWN* S43 ......9 F3
Braemar Cl *STV/CWN* S43 ......9 F3
Bramble Cl *BSVR* S44 ......41 F2
Brambling Ct *CHNE* S41 ......27 E3
Bramlyn Cl *STV/CWN* S43 ......13 H2
Bramlyn Ct *STV/CWN* S43 ......13 H2
Bramshill Ri *CHSW* S40 ......25 H4
Brandene Cl *STV/CWN* S43 ......28 A2
Branton Cl *CHSW* S40 ......26 B4
Brassington La *RCH* S42 ......39 E5
Brassington St *CLCR* S45 ......43 F2
Brearley Av *CHNE* S41 ......9 F4
Brearley St *CHNE* S41 ......9 E4
Breckland Rd *CHSW* S40 ......25 F5
Brecon Cl *CHSW* S40 ......17 G5
Brendon Av *CHSW* S40 ......25 F5
Brent Cl *CHSW* S40 ......2 B1
Bretby Rd *CHSW* S40 ......17 E4
Bretton Av *BSVR* S44 ......31 G4
Bretton Cl *CHSW* S40 ......17 E5
Brewery St *CHNE* S41 ......3 H5
Briar Briggs Rd *BSVR* S44 ......30 D2
Briardene Cl *RCH* S42 ......16 D3
Briar Vw *STV/CWN* S43 ......19 G3
Brickhouse Yd *CHSW* S40 ......2 C6
Bricky Cl *STV/CWN* S43 ......13 H2
Bridge Bank Cl *CHSW* S40 ......17 H4
Bridge St *CHSW* S40 ......26 C4
  CLCR S45 ......43 F1
  RCH S42 ......39 F2
Bridgewater St *RCH* S42 ......39 E2
Bridle Rd *BSVR* S44 ......13 F5
  STV/CWN S43 ......11 H5
Brierley Cl *STV/CWN* S43 ......21 E1
Brierley Rd *DRON* S18..............39 H4
Bright St *RCH* S42 ......39 H4
Brimington Rd *CHNE* S41 ......19 E5
Brimington Rd North
  CHNE S41 ......18 C2
Brincliffe Cl *CHSW* S40 ......25 F4
Brindley Cl *CHNE* S41 ......18 C4
Brindley Wy *STV/CWN* S43 ......11 F5
Britannia Rd *CHSW* S40 ......34 D1
Broadgorse Cl *CHSW* S40 ......34 B1
Broadoaks Cl *CHNE* S41 ......3 K7
Broad Pavement *CHSW* S40 ......3 H6
Brockley Av *BSVR* S44 ......22 D4
Brocklehurst Piece *CHSW* S40 ......2 A6
Brockley Av *BSVR* S44 ......22 D4
Brockwell La *RCH* S42 ......16 D3
Brockwell Pl *CHSW* S40 ......2 C3
Brockwell Ter *CHSW* S40 ......2 D3
Bromehead Wy *CHNE* S41 ......17 H3
Brookbank Av *CHSW* S40 ......2 B4
Brookbank Rd *STV/CWN* S43 ......14 B3
Brook Cl *RCH* S42 ......32 B1
Brooke Dr *STV/CWN* S43 ......19 H5
Brookfield Av *CHSW* S40 ......25 E3
Brookfield Pk
  CLCR (off Mill La) S45 ......42 B1
Brookfield Rd *BSVR* S44 ......31 E5
Brookhill *STV/CWN* S43 ......14 A3
Brook La *STV/CWN* S43 ......14 B3
Brooklyn Dr *CHSW* S40 ......2 B4

Brookside Bar *CHSW* S40 ....24 D3
Brookside Gln *CHSW* S40 ....24 D3
Brooks Rd *STV/CWN* S43 ....10 B3
Brook St *CLCR* S45 ....42 C2
Brook V
  CHSW (off Chatsworth Rd) S40 ......2 C7
Brook Vale Cl *DRON* S18 ....6 B4
Brookview Ct *DRON* S18 ....5 E1
Brook Yd
  CHSW (off Chatsworth Rd) S40 ......2 E6
Broombank Pk *DRON* S18 ....7 H4
Broombank Rd *DRON* S18 ....7 H4
Broom Cl *CHNE* S41 ....17 H3
Broom Dr *RCH* S42 ....39 C1
Broomfield Av *CHNE* S41 ....35 F1
Broom Gdns *STV/CWN* S43 ....19 H3
Broomhill Rd *CHNE* S41 ....8 B5
Brown La *DRON* S18 ....5 C1
Brunswick St *CHNE* S41 ....3 C3
Brushfield Rd *RCH* S42 ....16 D5
Bryn Lea *CHNE* S41 ....27 E3
Buckden Cl *DRON* S18 ....2 B3
Buckingham Cl *DRON* S18 ....4 B2
The Bungalows
  CHNE (off Piccadilly) S41 ....3 K7
  CHNE
  (off Brimington Rd North) S41 ......18 C2
  CHSW
  (off Barker La) S40 ....2 B6
  STV/CWN
  (off Barlborough Rd) S43 ....14 A2
Bunting Cl *CHSW* S40 ....25 F4
Burbage Cl *DRON* S18 ....4 B2
Burbage Rd *STV/CWN* S43 ....20 C3
Burgess Cl *CHNE* S41 ....35 F1
Burkitt Dr *STV/CWN* S43 ....11 H4
Burley Cl *CHSW* S40 ....34 C1
Burlington House
  CHSW (off Burlington St) S40 ......3 H6
Burlington St *CHSW* S40 ....3 H6
Burnaston Cl *DRON* S18 ....4 A3
Burnbridge Rd *CHNE* S41 ....9 E4
Burnell St *STV/CWN* S43 ....19 H2
Burns Cl *CHSW* S40 ....34 B1
Burns Dr *DRON* S18 ....5 C4
  RCH S42 ....35 C5
Burrs Wood Cft *CHSW* S40 ....17 F3
Bursdon Cl *CHNE* S41 ....18 C1
Buttermere Cl *CHNE* S41 ....17 H3
Buttermere Dr *DRON* S18 ....4 C3
Buttermilk La *BSVR* S44 ....30 A2
Butterton Dr *CHSW* S40 ....17 E5
Butt Hl *WRKS* S80 ....15 H1
Butt Hill Cl *WRKS* S80 ....15 H1
Byron Cl *DRON* S18 ....5 C5
  RCH S42 ....35 C5
Byron Rd *CHSW* S40 ....26 C5
Byron St *CHSW* S40 ....26 C4

C

Caernarvon Cl *CHSW* S40 ....25 G4
Caernarvon Rd *DRON* S18 ....5 E4
Cairn Dr *STV/CWN* S43 ....9 F3
Cairngorm Cl *STV/CWN* S43 ....9 F3
Caldey Rd *DRON* S18 ....5 E4
Callywhite La *DRON* S18 ....5 C5
Calow Brook Dr *CHNE* S41 ....27 G5
Calow La *BSVR* S44 ....27 G4
  CHNE S41 ....27 G5
Calver Av *RCH* S42 ....40 A4
Calver Crs *STV/CWN* S43 ....20 D3
Cambrian Cl *CHSW* S40 ....17 H4
Cambridge Rd *STV/CWN* S43 ....19 H2
Camerory Wy *STV/CWN* S43 ....9 F2
Campbell Cottages
  STV/CWN
  (off Whittington Rd) S43 ....10 A3
Campbell Ct
  STV/CWN (off Church Wk) S43 ......9 F3
Campbell Dr *STV/CWN* S43 ....10 B3
Canal Whf *CHNE* S41 ....3 J3
Candlins Yd
  STV/CWN (off High St) S43 ....13 H4
Cannell Cl *CLCR* S45 ....42 D2
Capel Ri *STV/CWN* S43 ....19 F2
Capthorne Cl *RCH* S42 ....16 D5
Carlisle Cl *CHNE* S41 ....8 A4
Carlton Cl *CLCR* S45 ....43 F4
Carlton Rd *CHSW* S40 ....34 B2
Carlyon Gdns *CHSW* S40 ....26 B5
Carnoustie Av *CHSW* S40 ....25 G5
Carpenter Av *STV/CWN* S43 ....11 H4
Carr La *DRON* S18 ....4 A2
Carr Vale Rd *BSVR* S44 ....30 D4
Carrwood Rd *DRON* S18 ....7 F4

Carsington Cl *CHSW* S40 ....17 F5
Cartmel Cl *DRON* S18 ....4 C3
Cartmel Crs *CHNE* S41 ....17 H2
Castle Bungalows
  BSVR (off Castle St) S44 ....31 E3
Castle Gn *BSVR* S44 ....31 F5
Castle La *BSVR* S44 ....30 D4
Castlerigg Wy *DRON* * S18 ....4 C3
Castle St *BSVR* S44 ....31 E3
Castleton Gv *STV/CWN* S43 ....20 B5
Castle Yd *CHSW* S40 ....3 G7
Catchford Vw *CHSW* * S40 ....17 F3
Catherine St *CHSW* S40 ....2 D6
Caudwell Cl *RCH* S42 ....39 F3
Cauldon Dr *CHSW* S40 ....17 E5
Cavell Dr *STV/CWN* S43 ....43 G4
Cavendish Cl *RCH* S42 ....41 E2
Cavendish Dr *STV/CWN* S43 ....14 C3
Cavendish Pl *STV/CWN* S43 ....10 B4
Cavendish Ri *DRON* S18 ....4 D4
Cavendish Rd *BSVR* S44 ....31 F5
Cavendish St *CHSW* S40 ....3 H6
  STV/CWN S43 ....20 C2
Cavendish St North *CHNE* S41 ......8 C5
Caxton Cl *CHNE* S41 ....9 F4
Cecil Av *DRON* S18 ....5 E2
Cecil Rd *DRON* S18 ....5 E1
Cedar Av *CHSW* S40 ....2 B2
Cedar Park Dr *BSVR* S44 ....31 G3
Cedar St *STV/CWN* S43 ....20 A1
Cemetery La *STV/CWN* S43 ....21 E1
Cemetery Rd *CHNE* S41 ....27 E3
  CLCR S45 ....43 F4
  DRON S18 ....5 F4
Cemetery Ter *STV/CWN* S43 ......19 G3
Central Cl *DRON* S18 ....8 A1
Central Dr *BSVR* S44 ....27 H2
  CHNE S41 ....27 E4•
  RCH S42 ....34 B5
Central Pavement *CHSW* * S40 ......3 H6
Central St *CHNE* S41 ....27 E4
  RCH S42 ....41 E3
Central Wk *STV/CWN* S43 ....19 F3
Chaddesden Cl *DRON* S18...........4 A3
Challands Cl *CHNE* S41 ....27 E5
Challands Wy *CHNE* S41 ....27 E5
Chander Hill La *RCH* S42 ....24 A4
Chaneyfield Wy *CHSW* S40 ....17 F3
Chantrey Av *CHNE* S41 ....18 B4
Chapel Cl *STV/CWN* S43 ....14 A3
Chapel La East *CHNE* S41 ....35 F1
Chapel La West *CHSW* S40 ....25 G3
Chapel Rd *BSVR* S44 ....30 D4
  RCH S42 ....35 G5
Chapel St *CHNE* S41 ....18 C2
  STV/CWN S43 ....19 H2
Chapel Yd *DRON* S18 ....5 E2
Chapman La *RCH* S42 ....35 G5
Charles St *CHSW* S40 ....2 D6
Charlesworth St *BSVR* S44 ....30 C5
Chartwell Av *RCH* S42 ....33 H3
Chasecliff Cl *CHSW* S40 ....2 A1
Chatsworth Av *CHSW* S40.........25 F3
Chatsworth Cl *BSVR* S44 ....31 G3
Chatsworth Ct *STV/CWN* S43 ......20 D2
Chatsworth Dr *RCH* S42 ....39 H5
Chatsworth Pl *DRON* S18 ....4 B2
Chatsworth Rd *CHSW* S40 ....2 C6
  CHSW S40 ....25 E3
Chaucer Dr *DRON* S18 ....5 C5
Chaucer Rd *CHNE* S41 ....18 B2
Chavery Rd *CLCR* S45 ....43 G2
Cheedale Cl *CHSW* S40 ....17 H4
Cheetham Av *DRON* S18 ....8 A2
Chepstow Cl *CHSW* S40 ....26 B5
Cherry Tree Dr *BSVR* S44 ....31 G4
Cherry Tree Dr *BSVR* S44 ....29 F1
Cherry Tree Gv *RCH* S42 ....43 H1
  STV/CWN S43 ....12 A4
Chertsey Cl *CHSW* S40 ....26 B5
Cherwell Cl *STV/CWN* S43 ....19 C1
Chesterfield Cl *STV/CWN* S43 ......9 G4
Chesterfield Rd *BSVR* S44 ....22 C5
  BSVR S44 ....28 B3
  CHNE S41 ....19 E4
  DRON S18 ....5 F3
  RCH S42 ....39 H3
  RCH S42 ....40 C1
  STV/CWN S43 ....13 E2
  STV/CWN S43 ....19 F3
Chester St *CHSW* S40 ....2 C5
Chesterton Cl *STV/CWN* S43 ......27 H1
Chestnut Cl *DRON* S18 ....5 F4
Chestnut Dr *STV/CWN* S43 ....13 H3
  WRKS S80 ....15 F5
Cheviot Wy *CHSW* S40 ....17 G5
Chigwell Wy *STV/CWN* S43 ....10 B4
Chiltern Cl *CHSW* S40 ....25 G1

RCH S42 ....35 H5
Chiverton Cl *DRON* S18 ....5 E2
Church Av *CLCR* S45 ....43 G3
Church Cl *RCH* S42 ....34 C4
  STV/CWN S43 ....14 B4
Church Houses
  STV/CWN (off Cedar St) S43 ......20 A1
Churchland Rd *RCH* S42 ....40 D3
Church La *BSVR* S44 ....27 H2
  BSVR S44 ....37 H5
  CHSW S40 ....3 H6
  RCH S42 ....36 B5
  RCH S42 ....43 H1
  STV/CWN S43 ....14 B4
Church La North *CHNE* S41...........8 C4
Church Mdw *BSVR* S44 ....27 H2
  RCH S42 ....43 H1
Church Paddock *RCH* S42............43 H1
Church Side *BSVR* S44 ....23 E4
Church Side *BSVR* S44 ....27 H2
Churchside La *CHNE* S41 ....35 F2
Churchside La *CHNE* S41 ....35 F2
Church St *BSVR* S44 ....27 H2
  BSVR S44 ....31 E4
  DRON S18 ....5 E3
  STV/CWN S43 ....11 E5
  STV/CWN S43 ....14 A4
  STV/CWN S43 ....19 G3
Church St North *CHNE* S41...........8 C4
Church St South *CHSW* S40 ......34 C1
Church St West *CHSW* S40 ....25 G3
Church Vw *STV/CWN* S43 ....25 G3
  STV/CWN S43 ....14 B4
Church Wy *CHSW* S40 ....3 H6
Churston Rd *CHSW* S40 ....2 A5
Circular Rd *CHNE* S41 ....26 D5
  STV/CWN S43 ....20 C2
Clarence Rd *CHSW* S40 ....3 F6
Clarence St *CHSW* S40 ....2 E6
Clarendon Rd *STV/CWN* S43 ......20 C3
Claylands Gv *STV/CWN* S43 ......15 G2
Claylands Pl *WRKS* S80 ....15 G2
Claylands Rd *WRKS* S80 ....15 G2
Clay La *CLCR* S45 ....42 D4
Clay Pit Wy *STV/CWN* S43 ....13 C1
Clayton St *CHNE* S41 ....26 D3
Cleveland Wy *CHSW* S40 ....25 F1
Cliff Hl *STV/CWN* S43 ....13 G4
Clifford Cl *CHSW* S40 ....25 F3
Clifton St *CHSW* S40 ....2 C6
The Clough *CHNE* S41 ....27 G4
Clowne Rd *BSVR* S44 ....23 E2
  STV/CWN S43 ....13 C1
Clubmill Ter *CHSW* S40 ....2 C3
Clumber Cl *STV/CWN* S43 ....14 B3
Clumber Pl *STV/CWN* S43 ....20 C4
Clune St *STV/CWN* S43 ....14 C2
Cobden Rd *CHSW* S40 ....3 F4
Cobnar Dr *CHNE* S41 ....17 H2
Colenso Pl
  RCH
  (off Queen Victoria Rd) S42 ......39 E2
College Av *STV/CWN* S43 ....20 D1
Colliers Trek *STV/CWN* S43 ......13 G2
Colliers Wy *CLCR* S45 ....42 D2
Colliery Cl *STV/CWN* S43 ....21 F1
Collishaw Cl *CHNE* S41 ....27 E5
Colton Cl *CHNE* S41 ....18 A1
Common La *RCH* S42 ....16 C1
Commonside Rd *DRON* S18 ......6 A5
Compass Crs *CHNE* S41 ....9 E4
Compton St *CHSW* S40 ....2 E4
  RCH S42 ....41 E2
Conduit Rd *BSVR* S44 ....31 E5
Coney Green Rd *CLCR* S45 ......43 G2
Coniston Dr *CLCR* S45 ....42 D3
Coniston Cl *CHNE* S41 ....17 H2
  DRON S18 ....4 C3
Coniston Wy *CHNE* S41 ....18 A2
Connelly Ct
  CHSW (off Chester St) S40 ......2 D5
Constable Cl *DRON* S18 ....4 C4
Cooke Cl *RCH* S42 ....38 D5
Copenhagen Rd *CLCR* S45 ......43 G2
Coppice Cl *CHNE* S41 ....35 F2
Coral Wy *CLCR* S45 ....43 F2
Cordwell Av *CHNE* S41 ....17 G2
Cordwell Cl *STV/CWN* S43 ....20 D2
Cornfield Cl *CHSW* S40 ....17 E5
Cornmill Cl *BSVR* S44 ....31 G3
Cornwall Av *STV/CWN* S43 ....19 H2
Cornwall Cl *STV/CWN* S43 ....19 H2
Cornwall Dr *RCH* S42 ....35 H5
  STV/CWN S43 ....19 H2
Coronation Rd *STV/CWN* S43 ......19 G2
Corporation St *CHNE* S41 ....3 J5
Corve Wy *RCH* S42 ....16 D5
Cotswold Dr *RCH* S42 ....35 G5

Cottage Cl *STV/CWN* S43 ....
Cottam Dr *STV/CWN* S43 ....
Cotterhill La *STV/CWN* S43 ....
Cotton Mill Hl *RCH* S42 ....
Cotton St *BSVR* S44 ....
Coupe La *CLCR* S45 ....
Coupland Cl *CHNE* S41 ....
Court Pl *STV/CWN* S43 ....
Court Vw *STV/CWN* S43 ....
Cow La *STV/CWN* S43 ....
Cowley Bottom *DRON* S18 ....
Cowley Cl *CHNE* S41 ....
Cowley La *DRON* S18 ....
Cowpingle La *STV/CWN* S43 ....
Cowsell Dr *CLCR* S45 ....
Craggon Dr *STV/CWN* S43 ....
Craggs Dr *STV/CWN* S43 ....
Craggs Rd *BSVR* S44 ....
Craglands Gv *RCH* S42 ....
Cranborne Rd *CHNE* S41 ....
Cranleigh Rd *STV/CWN* S43 ....
Craven Rd *CHNE* S41 ....
Crescent Rd *RCH* S42 ....
The Crescent *CLCR* S45 ....
  RCH S42 ....
  STV/CWN S43 ....
  STV/CWN S43 ....
Cressbrook Av *RCH* S42............
Creswell Rd *STV/CWN* S43 ....
Creswick Cl *CHSW* S40............
Crich Pl *RCH* S42............
Crich Rd *STV/CWN* S43............
Crich Vw *BSVR* S44............
Cricket Vw *STV/CWN* S43 ....
Croft Lea *DRON* S18 ....
Crofton Cl *DRON* S18 ....
Crofton Ri *DRON* S18 ....
Croft Vw *STV/CWN* S43 ....
  STV/CWN S43 ....
Cromarty Ri *DRON* S18 ....
Cromdale Av *STV/CWN* S43............
Cromford Cl *RCH* S42............
Cromford Dr *STV/CWN* S43............
Cromford Rd *CLCR* S45 ....
Crompton Rd *STV/CWN* S43 ....
Cromwell Rd *BSVR* S44 ....
  CHSW S40 ....
Cropston Cl *CHNE* S41 ....
Crossfield Vls
  BSVR (off Chesterfield Rd) S44 ......
  DRON S18 ....
Cross London St *STV/CWN* S43 ......
Cross St *BSVR* S44 ....
  CHSW S40 ....
  CLCR S45 ....
  RCH S42 ....
  RCH S42 ....
  STV/CWN S43 ....
Cross Wellington St
  STV/CWN * S43 ....
Crow La *CHNE* S41 ....
Crown Cl *CHNE* S41 ....
Crown Rd *CHNE* S41 ....
Crown St *STV/CWN* S43 ....
Cruck Cl *DRON* S18 ....
Cuckoo Wy *STV/CWN* S43 ....
  STV/CWN S43 ....
Cundy Rd *BSVR* S44 ....
Curbar Cl *RCH* S42 ....
Curbar Curve *STV/CWN* S43 ....
Curzon Av *DRON* S18 ....
Cuttholme Rd *CHSW* S40 ....
Cutthorpe Cft *RCH* S42 ....
Cutthorpe Rd *RCH* S42 ....

D

Dade Av *STV/CWN* S43............
Dale Bank Crs *CHNE* S41 ....
Dale Cl *STV/CWN* S43 ....
Dale Crs *RCH* S42 ....
Dale Rd *DRON* S18 ....
  RCH S42 ....
Dalewood Cl *CHNE* S41 ....
Dalvey Wy *STV/CWN* S43............
Damon Dr *STV/CWN* S43............
Damsbrook Dr *STV/CWN* S43 ....
Damsbrook La *BSVR* S44............
Danbury Gv *RCH* S42............
Danby Av *CHNE* S41 ....
Dark La *BSVR* S44 ....
  CHNE S41 ....
  RCH S42 ....
Darley Av *RCH* S42 ....
Darley Cl *STV/CWN* S43 ....

H

Hackney La *DRON* S18....................6 D5
Haddon Cl *CHSW* S40..............25 G3
   DRON S18................................5 F2
Haddon Pl *STV/CWN* S43.........20 D2
Haddon Rd *RCH* S42................40 A3
Hady Crs *CHNE* S41..................27 E2
Hady Hl *CHNE* S41....................27 E3
Hady La *CHNE* S41...................27 F3
Hague La *STV/CWN* S43............12 A1
Halcyon Ap *RCH* S42.................39 E1
Haldane Cl *WRKS* S80...............15 G5
Haldane Crs *BSVR* S44..............30 D3
Halesworth Cl *CHSW* S40..........25 F5
Half Acre La *DRON* S18..............5 H4
Half Cft *STV/CWN* S43...............19 H3
Hall Cl *DRON* S18......................4 A2
   RCH S42..............................16 C2
Hall Farm Cl *CHNE* S41.............35 F2
Hallfield Cl *RCH* S42................34 C4
Hallflash La *BSVR* S44..............28 A5
Hall La *STV/CWN* S43...............10 C3
Hallowes Ct *DRON* S18...............5 F3
Hallowes Dr *DRON* S18...............5 F4
Hallowes La *DRON* S18...............5 F4
Hallowes Ri *DRON* S18................5 G4
Hall Rd *STV/CWN* S43...............19 G3
Halls Rw
   CHSW (off Barker La) S40..........2 B7
Hall Vw *CHNE* S41....................18 A4
Halton Cl *CHNE* S41..................18 A1
Hambledon Cl *CHSW* S40..........17 G5
Hambleton Av *RCH* S42.............39 H5
Hamill Cl *RCH* S42....................39 H4
Hampton St *CHNE* S41..............35 F1
Hanbury Cl *CHSW* S40...............17 E5
   DRON S18..............................4 D3
Handby St *CHNE* S41.................27 F5
Handley Ct *STV/CWN* S43...........9 F3
Handley Rd *ECK/KIL* S21.............9 F1
   STV/CWN S43..........................9 F3
Hardhurst Rd *DRON* S18..............8 A2
Hardie Pl *STV/CWN* S43............20 D2
Hardwick Av *CHNE* S41...............9 F4
Hardwick Cl *DRON* S18...............5 F2
   RCH S42..............................41 E3
   STV/CWN S43........................14 C3
Hardwick Dr *BSVR* S44..............28 D2
Hardwick St *CHNE* S41...............3 H3
Hardwicks Yd
   CHSW (off Chatsworth Rd) S40....2 C7
Hardwick View Rd *RCH* S42........41 F3
Harehill Crs *RCH* S42................33 H4
Harehill Rd *CHSW* S40..............34 B1
Harewood Crs *CLCR* S45...........42 C1
   RCH S42..............................38 C5
Harlesthorpe Av *STV/CWN* S43...14 B3
Harlesthorpe La *STV/CWN* S43...14 A2
Harperhill Cl *CHSW* S40.............34 B1
Hartfield Cl *CHNE* S41...............34 D1
Hartington Ct *STV/CWN* S43.......14 C3
Hartington Rd *CHNE* S41............27 E3
   DRON S18..............................5 F2
Hartington Vw *STV/CWN* S43......11 F4
Hartland Wy *CHNE* S41..............18 C1
Hartside Cl *CHSW* S40.................2 B1
Harvest Wy *CHSW* S40...............17 E5
Harvey Ct *BSVR* S44.................30 D3
Harvey Rd *CHNE* S41................27 C3
Haslam Ct *RCH* S42.................41 E2
Hasland Rd *CHNE* S41...............26 D4
Hassocky La *BSVR* S44..............36 B3
Hassop Cl *CHSW* S40................17 C4
   DRON S18..............................5 E3
Hassop Rd *STV/CWN* S43..........11 F5
Hastings Cl *CHNE* S41...............17 H4
Hathaway Cl *RCH* S42...............38 D5
Hathern Cl *STV/CWN* S43..........27 H1
Hatton Cl *DRON* S18..................4 B4
Hatton Dr *CHSW* S40................17 F5
Hawking La *BSVR* S44................41 G4
Hawkshead Av *DRON* S18............4 B3
Hawksley Av *CHSW* S40...............2 D2
Hawthorn Av *STV/CWN* S43........12 A3
Hawthorn Cl *STV/CWN* S43.........13 H3
Hawthorne Av *DRON* S18.............5 E1
   WRKS S80............................15 F4
Hawthorne Cl *STV/CWN* S43........13 C1
Hawthorne St *CHSW* S40............11 E2
Hawthorn Hl *STV/CWN* S43.........11 F1
Hawthorn Wy *RCH* S42..............16 D5
Hayfield Cl *DRON* S18.................4 B3
   RCH S42..............................34 B5
   STV/CWN S43........................11 F4
Hayford Wy *STV/CWN* S43..........21 E1

Hazel Cl *DRON* S18.....................5 F4
Hazel Ct *DRON* S18.....................5 F4
Hazel Dr *CHSW* S40...................25 H5
   RCH S42..............................34 D5
Hazel Gv *STV/CWN* S43..............12 A3
Hazelhurst *CHNE* S41.................35 F2
Hazelmere Rd *WRKS* S80...........15 E5
Hazelwood Cl *DRON* S18.............4 A3
Hazlehurst Av *CHNE* S41.............3 H2
Hazlehurst La *CHNE* S41.............3 H2
Hazlewood Dr *STV/CWN* S43.......13 F1
Headland Cl *STV/CWN* S43.........19 G3
Heath Common *BSVR* S44..........37 H5
Heathcote Dr *CHNE* S41............27 G5
Heather Av *BSVR* S44.................41 F1
Heather Cl *BSVR* S44.................28 A2
Heather Gdns *CHNE* * S41..........35 G1
Heather Vale Cl *CHNE* * S41........35 G1
Heather Vale Rd *CHNE* S41.........35 G1
Heather Wy *RCH* S42.................32 B1
Heathfield Av *CHSW* S40..............2 B5
Heathfield Cl *DRON* S18...............5 E4
   RCH S42..............................34 D4
Heath Rd *RCH* S42....................41 E2
Heaton Cl *DRON* S18...................4 B3
Heaton St *CHSW* S40.................25 G3
Hedley Dr *STV/CWN* S43............19 F2
Helmsley Cl *CHSW* S40...............17 G3
Helston Cl *CHNE* S41.................26 D5
Henry St *CHNE* S41...................18 D2
   RCH S42..............................35 G5
Hereford Dr *STV/CWN* S43..........19 H2
Heritage Dr *STV/CWN* S43..........13 H3
Herriot Dr *CHSW* S40.................26 D4
Hewers Holt *STV/CWN* S43.........13 F1
Heywood St *STV/CWN* S43..........19 G2
Heywood Vw *STV/CWN* S43.........13 G1
Hickingwood La *STV/CWN* S43.....14 B2
Hickinwood Crs *STV/CWN* S43.....14 B2
Hides Gn *BSVR* S44..................31 E3
Highbury Rd *CHNE* S41................3 H2
Higher Albert St *CHNE* S41...........3 G3
Highfield Av *CHNE* S41.................2 C1
Highfield La *CHNE* S41...............18 A4
Highfield Rd *BSVR* S44..............31 E4
   CHNE S41..............................3 F1
Highfields Crs *DRON* S18.............5 E4
Highfields Dr *RCH* S42...............40 D3
Highfields Rd *DRON* S18..............5 E4
Highfields Wy *RCH* S42..............40 D3
Highfield Ter
   CHNE (off Highfield Rd) S41.........3 F2
Highfield View Rd *CHNE* S41.........3 F1
Highgate Dr *DRON* S18................5 G5
Highgate La *DRON* S18................5 G5
High Hazels Cl *CLCR* S45............43 G2
High Hazels Rd *STV/CWN* S43.....13 E2
Highland Rd *STV/CWN* S43...........9 F2
High La *RCH* S42......................32 C3
High Leys Rd *STV/CWN* S43........14 A5
Highlow *STV/CWN* S43...............17 G5
High St *BSVR* S44....................31 E4
   CHNE S41..............................8 C5
   CHSW S40..............................3 G6
   CLCR S45.............................43 E3
   DRON S18..............................4 D2
   STV/CWN S43........................11 E5
   STV/CWN S43........................13 H4
   STV/CWN S43........................19 H2
   WRKS S80............................15 H1
High View Cl *CHNE* S41..............27 F5
Highwood La *WRKS* S80.............15 E1
Hillberry Ri *RCH* S42.................34 B2
Hillcrest Gv *STV/CWN* S43..........11 F4
Hillcrest Rd *CHNE* S41...............35 F1
Hill Gv *STV/CWN* S43.................10 B3
Hillhouses La *RCH* S42..............34 A5
Hillman Dr *STV/CWN* S43...........20 C4
Hillside *WRKS* S80....................15 H2
Hillside Av *DRON* S18..................5 E4
Hillside Cl *WRKS* S80.................15 H2
Hillside Dr *CHNE* S41.................25 H4
   STV/CWN S43........................12 A4
Hill St *CLCR* S45......................43 E3
Hill Top *BSVR* S44....................31 E3
Hilltop Rd *CHNE* S41...................8 D5
   DRON S18..............................5 E4
   RCH S42..............................33 H4
Hilltop Wy *DRON* S18..................5 E5
Hill View Rd *STV/CWN* S43..........19 G2
Hipley Cl *CHSW* S40..................17 F5
Hipper St *CHSW* S40....................3 H7
Hipper St South *CHSW* S40...........3 H7
Hipper St West *CHSW* S40............2 C7
Hoades St *RCH* S42..................39 E3
Hockley La *RCH* S42..................38 C1
Hoggarth Ri *DRON* S18................4 D3
Holbeach Dr *CHSW* S40.............26 A5

Holbeck Av *BSVR* S44................31 G3
Holbeck Cl *CHNE* S41..................3 J4
Holbein Cl *DRON* S18...................4 D4
Holbrook Av *RCH* S42................40 A4
Holbrook Cl *CHSW* S40..............25 G5
Holbrook Pl *STV/CWN* S43..........20 C3
Holburn Av *DRON* S18.................5 E2
Holland Rd *CHNE* S41..................8 B5
Hollens Wy *RCH* S42.................16 D5
Hollies Cl *DRON* S18...................5 G4
Hollin Cl *CHNE* S41...................17 G2
Hollingwood Crs *STV/CWN* S43....20 A1
Hollin Hl *STV/CWN* S43..............14 C4
Hollins Spring Av *DRON* S18.........5 E4
Hollins Spring Rd *DRON* S18.........5 E4
Hollis La *CHNE* S41.....................3 J7
   CHSW S40..............................3 J7
Hollythorpe Cl *CHNE* S41............27 F5
Holmebank Cl *CHSW* S40.............2 C4
Holme Bank East *CHSW* S40.........2 C4
Holmebank Vw *CHSW* S40............2 C4
Holme Bank West *CHSW* S40........2 C4
Holmebrook Vw *CHSW* S40.........17 G4
Holme Hall Crs *CHSW* S40..........17 F5
Holme Park Av *CHSW* S40..........17 F3
Holme Rd *CHNE* S41..................18 C4
Holmesdale Cl *DRON* S18.............5 G1
Holmesdale Rd *DRON* S18............5 F1
Holmgate Rd *CLCR* S45.............42 A3
Holmley Bank *DRON* S18..............5 E1
Holmley La *DRON* S18..................5 E1
Holymoor Rd *RCH* S42...............32 B1
Holywell St *CHNE* S41..................3 H5
Homeport Ms *CHNE* S41..............3 H3
Hoodcroft La *BSVR* S44..............13 E5
Hoole St *CHNE* S41...................27 F5
Hope St *CHSW* S40.....................2 C6
Hornscroft Rd *BSVR* S44............31 E4
Horsehead La *BSVR* S44.............31 F3
Horsewood Rd *CHSW* S40..........25 F5
Horsley Cl *CHSW* S40................17 E5
Houfton Crs *BSVR* S44...............30 D2
Houfton Rd *BSVR* S44................30 D2
Houldsworth Crs *BSVR* S44.........30 D3
Houldsworth Dr *CHNE* S41..........27 G3
Howard Dr *CHNE* S41...................8 C5
   RCH S42..............................43 H1
Howden Cl *STV/CWN* S43...........11 F5
Howells Pl *STV/CWN* S43............11 H4
Hoylake Av *CHSW* S40...............33 C1
Hucklow Av *CHSW* S40...............26 B4
   RCH S42..............................40 A3
   STV/CWN S43........................20 C3
Hucknall Av *CHSW* S40...............25 G1
Hudson Mt *BSVR* S44................31 F5
Hundall La *CHNE* S41...................8 C3
Hunloke Av *CHSW* S40...............25 H4
Hunloke Crs *CHSW* S40..............26 A4
Hunloke Rd *RCH* S42.................41 E2
Hunloke Vw *RCH* S42.................34 D4
Huntingdon Av *BSVR* S44............31 F4
Huntley Cl *STV/CWN* S43............20 B2
Huntsman Rd *STV/CWN* S43.......11 E5
Hutchings Crs *STV/CWN* S43.......13 H2
Hyndley Rd *BSVR* S44................30 D2

I

Ians Wy *CHSW* S40...................25 G1
Ilam Cl *STV/CWN* S43................20 C4
Infirmary Rd *CHNE* S41................3 J3
Ingleby Cl *DRON* S18...................4 A3
Ingleton Rd *CHNE* S41................34 D1
Inkerman Cottages
   CHSW (off Ashgate Rd) S40.......25 G2
Inkersall Green Rd *STV/CWN* S43...20 B2
Inkersall Rd *STV/CWN* S43..........21 E4
Intake Rd *BSVR* S44..................30 C2
Ireland Cl *STV/CWN* S43.............21 F1
Ireland St *STV/CWN* S43.............11 F5
Iron Cliff Rd *BSVR* S44...............30 D2
Irongate *CHSW* S40.....................3 H6
Ivan Brook Cl *DRON* * S18............4 A3
Ivanhoe Cl *RCH* S42.................39 F2
Ivy Cl *CHNE* S41........................8 C5
Ivy Spring Cl *RCH* S42...............34 D4

J

Jackson Av *RCH* S42.................39 E3
Jackson Rd *CLCR* S45...............43 G3
Jago Av *STV/CWN* S43...............14 C3
James St *CHNE* S41..................18 C4
Jebb Gdns *CHSW* S40...............25 G3

Jepson Rd *CHNE* S41....................
Jervis Pl *STV/CWN* S43.................
Johnstone Cl *CHSW* S40................
John St *CHSW* S40.......................
   CLCR S45..............................
   RCH S42...............................
   STV/CWN S43..........................
   STV/CWN S43..........................
Joseph Fletcher Dr *RCH* S42.........
Jubilee Crs *STV/CWN* S43.............
Jubilee Gdns *WRKS* S80..............
Jubilee Pl *WRKS* S80..................
Jubilee Rd *WRKS* S80.................

K

Keats Rd *CHNE* S41.....................
Keats Wy *RCH* S42......................
Kedleston Cl *CHSW* S40...............
Keepers La *DRON* S18.................
Keilder Ct *CHSW* S40..................
Kelburn Av *CHSW* S40.................
Kendal Dr *DRON* S18...................
Kendal Rd *CHNE* S41...................
Kenmere Cl *CLCR* S45.................
Kennet V *CHNE* S41....................
Kenning St *CLCR* S45..................
Kent Cl *CHNE* S41......................
Kentmere Cl *DRON* S18...............
Kent St *CHNE* S41......................
Kenyon Rd *CHNE* S41..................
Keswick Cl *BSVR* S44..................
Keswick Dr *CHNE* S41.................
Keswick Pl *DRON* S18..................
Kidsley Cl *CHSW* S40..................
Kilburn Rd *DRON* S18..................
Kinder Rd *STV/CWN* S43..............
Kings Cl *STV/CWN* S43................
Kingsley Av *CHSW* S40................
Kingsmede Av *CHSW* S40............
King St *CLCR* S45.......................
   STV/CWN S43..........................
   STV/CWN S43..........................
King St North *CHNE* S41..............
King St South *CHNE* S40..............
Kingswood Cl *CHNE* S41..............
Kipling Cl *DRON* S18...................
Kipling Rd *CHNE* S41..................
Kirkdale Cl *CHSW* S40.................
Kirkstone Rd *CHNE* S41...............
Knifesmithgate *CHSW* S40............
Knighton St *RCH* S42..................
The Knoll *CHSW* S40...................
   DRON S18..............................

L

Laburnum Cl *BSVR* S44................
Laburnum Ct *BSVR* S44...............
Laburnum St *STV/CWN* S43..........
Ladybower La *STV/CWN* S43.........
Ladywood Dr *CHSW* S40..............
Lake Lands *RCH* S42...................
Lakeside *RCH* S42......................
Lakeside Cl *CHNE* S41.................
Lake View Av *CHSW* S40..............
Lancaster Rd *CHNE* S41...............
Lancelot Cl *CHSW* S40.................
Landsdowne Av *CHNE* S41...........
Landseer Cl *DRON* S18................
Langdale Cl *RCH* S42..................
Langdale Dr *DRON* S18................
Langdale Sq *STV/CWN* S43..........
Langer Field Av *CHSW* S40...........
Langer La *CHSW* S40..................
   RCH S42...............................
Langhurst Rd *CHSW* S40.............
Langley Cl *STV/CWN* S43.............
Langstone Av *BSVR* S44..............
Langtree Av *CHNE* S41................
Langwith Rd *BSVR* S44...............
Lansbury Av *STV/CWN* S43..........
Lansdowne Rd *STV/CWN* S43.......
Larch Wy *CHNE* S41....................
Lathkill Av *STV/CWN* S43.............
Lathkill Gv *CLCR* S45..................
Laurel Av *BSVR* S44...................
Laurel Crs *STV/CWN* S43.............
Laurel Garth Cl *CHNE* S41...........
Laurence Cl *CHNE* S41................
The Lawn *DRON* S18...................
Lawn Vls *BSVR* S44....................
Lawrence Av *RCH* S42................
Laxfield Cl *CHSW* S40.................

... CHNE S41 ....**18** D1
Rd *DRON* S18.....................**4** A3
ff Chesterfield Rd) S44 ......**30** B3
t
N (off Lowgates) S43..........**11** F5
RON S18...........................**5** E3
HNE S41 ....**27** G3
d CLHE S41 ....**17** H2
RCH S42 ....**39** H4
y CHNE S41 ....**18** A2
l CHSW S40 ....**2** B1
HSW S40 ....**25** G5
SVR S44 ....**41** F1
SVR S44 ....**31** G4
TV/CWN S43 ....**20** A1
l Cl RCH S42 ....**34** B2
STV/CWN S43 ....**21** E1
SVR S44 ....**28** A2
t Wy CLCR S45 ....**34** C5
Fields Rd BSVR S44 ....**31** E3
Wy CHNE S41 ....**13** F1
Cl STV/CWN S43 ....**19** H5
e Gv BSVR S44 ....**28** D2
... .**43** G4
v CLCR S45 ....**43** F4
ad CHSW S40 ....**25** E1
HSW S40 ....**26** C5
Wy RCH S42 ....**39** H5
d CHNE S41 ....**17** H2
v CHSW S40 ....**25** F4
... .**43** F4
S18 ....**5** F1
t CLCR S45 ....**43** F4
e La CHNE S41 ....**35** G2
ark Gv CHSW S40 ....**2** C5
ne Ct CHSW S40 ....**25** G4
ne Rd DRON S18 ....**5** E3
Gdns CHSW S40 ....**25** G5
HSW S40 ....**25** H5
s RCH S42..........................**40** A3
l DRON S18........................**5** E4
Cl CHNE S41 ....**17** H3
l CHSW S40 ....**25** G5
nd Rd CHSW S40 ....**17** F3
or CHNE S41 ....**17** H3
or Crs CHNE S41 ....**17** H3
orton Rd RCH S42 ....**39** H5
...CWN S43..........................**20** C2
rd La CHNE S41 ....**18** C4
l STV/CWN S43 ....**28** A1
r RCH S42 ....**34** C4
arm Cl CHSW S40 ....**33** G1
l STV/CWN S43 ....**20** C4
an St CHNE S41 ....**9** F4
e Rd DRON S18....................**5** E5
f Wk CHSW S40 ....**17** G4
urse La BSVR S44 ....**29** G3
oft Cl RCH S42 ....**39** F3
oft Crs DRON S18..................**4** A2
oft Rd DRON S18 ....**4** A2
oft Vw WRKS S80 ....**15** H1
ge Gv RCH S42 ....**34** D5
ge Gv BSVR S44 ....**34** B5
ge Ri RCH S42 ....**34** C4
ld Gra CHSW S40 ....**17** G4
rst Vw WRKS S80 ....**15** H2
nds BSVR S44 ....**31** F3
f Wk CHSW S40 ....**17** G4
aw Cl RCH S42 ....**39** H5
...CWN S43..........................**20** D3
oberts Rd CHSW S40 ....**20** C4
l BSVR S44 ....**31** E4
ill St CHSW S40 ....**3** J6
... .**34** B2
s Rd DRON S18 ....**8** A1
s Wood Av CHSW S40 ....**17** G4
ley Green Rd CHSW S40 .....**25** F1
Grove Rd CHSW S40.............**3** F6
Mantle Cl CLCR S45 ....**43** F2
ds STV/CWN S43 ....**11** G5
tes STV/CWN S43 ....**11** F5
vement CHSW S40 ....**3** H6
... .**13** F5
Dr DRON S18........................**4** D3
Cl CHSW S40 ....**25** F2
d CHNE S41 ....**2** D1
m Cl CHNE S41 ....**18** B3
ale Rd STV/CWN S43 ....**20** C4
DRON S18..............................**5** E4
Wy BSVR S44 ....**28** A2
s Cl STV/CWN S43 ....**19** G2
d Av CHNE S41.....................**18** D1
e Dr RCH S42 ....**34** A5
l STV/CWN S43 ....**43** G3
od Cl DRON S18....................**4** B3

M

MacDonald Cl *RCH* S42 ....**35** H5
Machins Ct *DRON* S18 ....**5** E2
Madin Dr *STV/CWN* S43 ....**20** B4
Madin St *CHNE* S41 ....**3** C3
RCH S42 ....**39** E3
Main Rd *BSVR* S44 ....**41** C1
RCH S42 ....**16** C3
Main St *BSVR* S44 ....**30** D5
Malham Cl *CHSW* S40 ....**2** B1
Malia Rd *CHNE* S41 ....**19** E4
Malkin St *CHNE* S41 ....**3** J5
Mallard Ct
    STV/CWN (off Lowgates) S43........**11** F5
Mallory Cl *DRON* S18 ....**18** A4
Malson Wy *CHNE* S41 ....**18** B4
Malthouse La *RCH* S42 ....**33** F5
Malvern Rd *CHSW* S40.................**2** D4
Manifold Av *STV/CWN* S43 ....**20** D2
Manknell Rd *CHNE* S41 ....**18** C2
Manor Av *STV/CWN* S43 ....**19** H3
Manor Ct *STV/CWN* S43 ....**14** B4
Manor Court Rd *BSVR* S44 ....**30** D2
Manor Crs *CHSW* S40...................**2** A6
    DRON S18.............................**4** D3
Manor Dr *CHSW* S40....................**2** A5
    STV/CWN S43 ....**19** H3
Manor Rd *CHSW* S40....................**2** A6
    CHSW S40 ....**25** G2
    STV/CWN S43 ....**19** H3
Mansfeldt Crs *CHNE* S41 ....**18** A4
Mansfeldt Rd *CHNE* S41 ....**18** A4
Mansfield Rd *BSVR* S44 ....**23** H4
    BSVR S44 ....**37** F5
    CHNE S41 ....**35** F1
    RCH S42 ....**36** A4
Manvers Rd *STV/CWN* S43 ....**28** A1
Maple Dr *WRKS* S80 ....**15** C5
Maple St *STV/CWN* S43 ....**20** B2
Mapperley Rd *DRON* S18 ....**4** A3
Marchwood Cl *CHSW* S40.............**2** D4
Mardale Cl *CHNE* S41 ....**18** A1
Market Pl *BSVR* S44 ....**31** E4
    CHSW S40 ....**3** G6
Market St *CLCR* S45 ....**43** F2
    STV/CWN S43 ....**11** E5
Markham Crs *STV/CWN* S43 ......**11** F5
Markham La *BSVR* S44 ....**29** H1
Markham Ri *CLCR* S45 ....**42** D2
Markham Rd *BSVR* S44 ....**21** H5
    CHSW S40 ....**3** F7
Markland Av *STV/CWN* S43 ....**14** C3
Markland Crs *STV/CWN* S43 ......**14** C3
Markland La *WRKS* S80 ....**14** C4
Markland Vw *WRKS* S80 ....**15** F4
Marlpit La *BSVR* S44 ....**31** C3
Marsden Pl
    CHNE (off Newbold Rd) S41 ....**3** G4
    CHSW (off Old Rd) S40 ....**2** B7
Marsden St *STV/CWN* S43 ....**5** F1
Marsh Av *DRON* S18 ....**5** F1
Marshfield Gv *STV/CWN* S43.......**11** G5
Marston Cl *DRON* S18 ....**4** B4
Martins La *RCH* S42 ....**38** D3
Marx Ct
    CLCR (off Bestwood Pk) S45 ....**43** E3
Mary Ann St *DRON* S18 ....**8** A3
Masefield Av *RCH* S42 ....**40** D1
Mason St *WRKS* S80 ....**15** H1
Masson Cl *CHSW* S40 ....**2** B1
Mastin Av *STV/CWN* S43 ....**13** G2
Mather's Wy *RCH* S42 ....**39** F2
Matlock Dr *STV/CWN* S43 ....**20** C5
May Av *CHNE* S41 ....**9** E4
Mayfield Dr *RCH* S42 ....**39** H5
Mayfield Rd *CHSW* S40 ....**25** C3
Maynard Rd *CHSW* S40 ....**26** B4
Mcgregor's Wy *CHSW* S40 ....**34** D2
Mcmahon Av *STV/CWN* S43 ....**20** B4
Meadow Cl *BSVR* S44 ....**31** E5
    CHNE S41 ....**9** F5
Meadow Cft *RCH* S42 ....**40** D3
Meadowlands *BSVR* S44 ....**31** C3
Meadow Ri *CHSW* S40 ....**24** D1
Meadow Rd *CLCR* S45 ....**42** C7
Meadows Dr *STV/CWN* S43 ....**21** F2
Meadowside Cl *RCH* S42 ....**34** C4
The Meadows *RCH* S42 ....**16** D5
Meadow Vw *CHSW* S40 ....**25** E5
    RCH S42 ....**40** D4
    STV/CWN S43 ....**14** B4
Meakin St *CHNE* S41 ....**27** F5
Medlock Rd *CHSW* S40 ....**25** G5
Melling Cl *CHSW* S40 ....**26** B5
Melling Cl *CHSW* S40 ....**26** B5

Mellor Wy *CHSW* S40 ....**34** C1
Melrose Cl *CHSW* S40 ....**25** G2
Meltham La *CHNE* S41 ....**18** D4
Melville Crs *STV/CWN* S43 ....**27** H1
Mendip Crs *CHSW* S40 ....**25** F1
Mercaston Cl *CHSW* S40 ....**17** E5
Merrian Cft
    STV/CWN
    (off Devonshire Av North) S43 ......**9** G4
Merrick Cl *CHSW* S40 ....**2** A1
Meynell Cl *RCH* S42 ....**25** C3
Michael Cl *RCH* S42 ....**34** C3
Middlecroft Rd *STV/CWN* S43 ....**20** C3
Middle La *CLCR* S45 ....**43** C3
Middle Pavement *CHSW * S40.......**3** G6
Middle Rd *RCH* S42 ....**38** A2
Middle St *BSVR* S44 ....**31** C5
Middleton Dr *STV/CWN* S43 ....**20** B5
Middletown Mdw
    STV/CWN S43 ....**13** E1
Midland Ct
    CHNE (off Storforth La) S41 .....**34** D1
Midland Ter
    CHNE (off Storforth La) S41 .....**34** D1
Midland Vw *RCH* S42 ....**39** H4
Midland Wy *STV/CWN* S43 ....**13** E2
Mile Hi
    CHNE (off Mansfield Rd) S41 ....**35** H3
Milford Rd *STV/CWN* S43 ....**20** C5
Milking La *STV/CWN* S43 ....**13** F4
Mill Crs *RCH* S42 ....**35** E5
Millcross La *DRON* S18...............**6** C4
Milldale Cl *CHSW* S40 ....**17** G5
Millennium Wy *CHNE* S41 ....**18** A1
Miller Av *STV/CWN* S43 ....**12** A3
Mill Gn *STV/CWN* S43 ....**10** D5
Mill Hi *BSVR* S44 ....**37** H2
Mill La *BSVR* S44 ....**22** D2
    BSVR S44 ....**31** E2
    BSVR S44 ....**41** H1
    CHSW S40 ....**2** B7
    CLCR S45 ....**42** B1
    CLCR S45 ....**42** D1
    DRON S18..............................**5** F3
Millstone Cl *DRON* S18 ....**4** B2
Mill Stream Cl *CHSW* S40 ....**25** G4
Mill St *CHNE* S41 ....**3** J6
    DRON S18..............................**5** E4
    STV/CWN S43 ....**14** A3
Mill Wk *BSVR* S44 ....**31** E2
Milton Crs *CHSW* S40 ....**26** C5
Milton Pl *STV/CWN* S43 ....**21** F1
Minimum Ter *CHSW* S40 ....**34** C1
Miriam Av *RCH* S42 ....**25** E5
Mitchell St *STV/CWN* S43 ....**14** B3
Mitchell Wy *STV/CWN* S43 ....**9** G4
Mods La
    DRON (off Commonside Rd) S18......**6** B4
Molineux Av *STV/CWN* S43 ....**20** D1
Monkwood Rd *CHNE* S41 ....**17** H2
Monnies End *STV/CWN* S43 ....**13** G2
Monsal Crs *STV/CWN* S43 ....**20** B4
Montrose Pl *DRON* S18 ....**4** B2
Monyash Cl *STV/CWN* S43 ....**20** C3
Moonpenny Wy *DRON* S18...........**5** E3
Moore Cl *RCH* S42 ....**40** D2
Moorfield Av *BSVR* S44 ....**31** F4
Moorfield Sq *BSVR* S44 ....**31** F4
Moorgate Crs *DRON* S18..............**5** F4
Moorhay *CHSW* S40 ....**17** H3
Moorland Dr *BSVR* S44 ....**41** F1
Moorland View Rd *CHSW* S40 ....**25** G4
Moor La *BSVR* S44 ....**28** C5
    BSVR S44 ....**31** F4
Moorlawn Av *RCH* S42 ....**40** C3
Moorpark Av *CHSW* S40 ....**25** G5
Moorview Cl *RCH* S42 ....**34** C5
    STV/CWN S43 ....**19** F3
Moor View Rd *STV/CWN* S43 .....**11** G5
Moray Pl *DRON* S18 ....**4** B2
Morley Av *CHSW* S40 ....**25** G1
Morley Cl *DRON* S18.....................**4** A3
Mornington Rd *RCH* S42 ....**40** D4
Morris Av *CHNE* S41 ....**18** A3
Morris Dr *CHNE* S41 ....**18** A3
Morton Av *CLCR* S45 ....**42** D2
Morven Av *BSVR * S44.................**51** H4
Mound Rd *CHSW* S40 ....**26** C4
Mountcastle St *CHNE * S41 ....**18** B2
Mount Pleasant
    CHNE (off Church St North) S41 ......**8** C4
Muirfield Cl *RCH* S42 ....**18** D4
Mulberry Cl *RCH* S42 ....**34** C4
Musard Pl *STV/CWN* S43 ....**20** D1
Myrtle Gv *STV/CWN* S43 ....**20** A1

N

Nairn Dr *DRON* S18.......................**4** B3
Neale Bank *STV/CWN* S43 ....**19** F3
Neale St *STV/CWN* S43 ....**14** B3
Nelson St *CHNE* S41 ....**18** C4
Nesbit St *BSVR* S44 ....**31** F5
Nesfield Cl *CHNE* S41 ....**17** H2
Nether Cl *RCH* S42 ....**38** C1
Nethercroft La *CLCR* S45 ....**43** G3
Nether Croft Rd *STV/CWN* S43....**19** G3
Netherdene Rd *DRON* S18 ....**5** E3
Netherfield Cl *STV/CWN* S43 ......**11** G5
Netherfield Rd *CHSW* S40 ....**25** E5
Netherfields Crs *DRON* S18 ....**5** E4
Netherleigh Rd *CHSW* S40 ....**25** F2
Nethermoor Rd *RCH* S42 ....**38** B1
    RCH S42 ....**39** E4
Nether Springs Rd *BSVR* S44 .....**30** D2
Netherthorpe *STV/CWN* S43........**11** G5
Netherthorpe Cl *STV/CWN* S43 ..**21** F1
Netherthorpe Rd *STV/CWN* S43...**11** F5
Nevis Cl *CHSW* S40 ....**2** A3
New Barlborough Cl
    STV/CWN S43 ....**13** H2
New Beetwell St *CHSW* S40 ....**3** C6
Newbold Av *CHNE* S41 ....**18** A4
Newbold Back La *CHSW* S40 ....**2** A4
Newbold Dr *CHNE* S41 ....**3** F3
Newbold Rd *CHNE* S41 ....**3** F3
    RCH S42 ....**17** E2
Newbridge Ct *STV/CWN* S43 ......**18** C1
Newbridge Dr *STV/CWN* S43 ......**19** F2
Newbridge La *CHNE* S41 ....**18** D1
    STV/CWN S43 ....**17** G2
Newby Rd *CHNE* S41 ....**17** G2
New Hall Rd *CHSW* S40 ....**2** A7
Newhaven Cl *CHSW* S40 ....**25** F4
Newland Dl *CHNE* S41 ....**3** H3
Newland Gdns *CHNE* S41 ....**2** D1
Newlands Av *CHSW* S40 ....**25** G2
Newmarket La *CLCR* S45 ....**42** A3
New Queen St *CHNE* S41 ....**3** F3
New Rd *RCH* S42 ....**32** B2
    RCH S42 ....**34** A5
New Station Rd *BSVR* S44 ....**30** D4
Newstead Cl *DRON* S18 ....**4** A3
New St *BSVR* S44 ....**31** E2
    CHSW S40 ....**26** C3
    RCH S42 ....**35** G5
    RCH S42 ....**39** H5
    WRKS S80 ....**15** G2
Newtons Croft Crs
    STV/CWN S43 ....**13** F1
Nicholas St *CHNE* S41 ....**35** F1
Nightingale Cl *CLCR* S45 ....**43** G4
Nobel Cl *WRKS* S80 ....**15** F4
Nook La *BSVR* S44 ....**28** B2
Norbriggs Rd *STV/CWN* S43 ......**12** A5
Norbury Cl *CHSW* S40 ....**17** F5
    DRON S18..............................**4** B3
Norfolk Av *RCH* S42 ....**39** H1
Norfolk Cl *CHSW* S40 ....**25** F5
North Cl *DRON* S18.......................**8** A1
North Crs *BSVR* S44 ....**21** G4
Northfields *STV/CWN* S43 ....**14** B4
North Gv *BSVR* S44 ....**21** G4
North La *RCH* S42 ....**16** B5
Northmoor Cl *STV/CWN * S43 .....**19** H3
North Moor Vw *STV/CWN* S43 ....**19** H3
North Rd *BSVR* S44 ....**27** H2
    STV/CWN S43 ....**14** A3
North Side *RCH* S42 ....**39** E2
North St *CLCR* S45 ....**42** C1
    RCH S42 ....**39** C5
North Ter
    CHNE (off Storforth La) S41.......**34** D1
North View *BSVR* S44 ....**30** C4
North Wingfield Rd *CHNE* S41 ....**35** G4
Norton Av *BSVR* S44 ....**22** D4
    RCH S42 ....**25** E5
Norwood Av *CHNE* S41 ....**35** F1
Norwood Cl *CHNE* S41 ....**35** G2
Nottingham Cl *RCH* S42 ....**34** D5
Nottingham Dr *RCH* S42 ....**34** D5
Nursery Dr *BSVR* S44 ....**30** D3

O

Oadby Dr *CHNE* S41 ....**35** E1
Oak Bank Av *CHNE* S41 ....**8** D4
Oak Cl *STV/CWN* S43 ....**19** F3
Oak Crs *RCH* S42 ....**34** B5
Oakdale Cl *CLCR* S45 ....**43** F4

Oakdell DRON S18 5 H1
Oakfield Av CHSW S40 25 F4
Oakhill Rd DRON S18 5 G2
Oaklea Wy RCH S42 38 D5
Oakley Av CHSW S40 2 D4
Oak Rd RCH S42 35 H5
Oaks Farm La BSVR S44 28 A3
Oak St STV/CWN S43 20 A1
Oak Tree Cl BSVR S44 28 D2
Oak Tree Rd STV/CWN S43 14 A5
Occupation Cl STV/CWN S43 13 E1
Occupation La RCH S42 39 G5
Occupation Rd CHNE S41 18 B2
Offridge Cl STV/CWN S43 14 B5
Old Bakery Cl CHNE S41 8 C5
Old Colliery La RCH S42 41 E3
Old Hall La WRKS S80 15 H1
Old Hall Rd CHSW S40 2 A7
Old Hl BSVR S44 31 E3
Old House Rd CHSW S40 17 H4
Old Mill Dr RCH S42 17 E3
Old Peverel Rd BSVR S44 21 G5
Old Quarry Cl STV/CWN S43 13 F1
Oldridge Cl CHSW S40 17 E4
Old Rd CHSW S40 2 B7
CHSW S40 25 E2
CHSW S40 25 G2
Old School La BSVR S44 27 H3
Old Ship La CHSW S40 3 H7
Old Whittington La DRON S18 8 A1
Orchard Cl BSVR S44 31 F4
STV/CWN S43 14 A4
Orchard Dr WRKS S80 15 G5
Orchard Sq DRON S18 4 B2
Orchards Wy CHSW S40 25 G4
Orchard Vw BSVR S44 30 C5
Orchard View Rd CHSW S40 25 G1
Orchid Cl BSVR S44 28 A2
Ormesby Cl DRON S18 4 A3
Ormond Cl CHSW S40 33 F1
Ormsby Rd CHNE S41 18 B3
Out La BSVR S44 41 E5
Outram Rd CHNE S41 18 B4
Overlees DRON S18 6 B4
Overton Cl STV/CWN S43 11 F4
Owlcotes Vw BSVR S44 31 E5
Ox Cl
CLCR (off Market St) S45 43 F2
Oxclose Dr DRON S18 4 A3
Oxclose La DRON S18 4 A3
Oxcroft La BSVR S44 31 F2
Oxford Cl STV/CWN S43 19 H2
Oxford Rd STV/CWN S43 19 H2

P

Packer's Rw CHSW S40 3 H6
Paddock Cl RCH S42 34 B5
The Paddocks STV/CWN S43 12 A4
The Paddock BSVR S44 31 F4
Paddock Wy DRON S18 5 F2
Padley Wy RCH S42 43 H1
Paisley Cl STV/CWN S43 20 C2
Palmer Crs DRON S18 5 F3
Palterton La BSVR S44 37 G2
Park Av DRON S18 5 F2
Park Cl CHSW S40 34 C1
Park Dr CHNE S41 26 D4
Parker Av STV/CWN S43 27 H2
Park Farm DRON S18 4 A2
Parkgate La ECK/KIL S21 9 G2
Park Hall Av CHSW S40 25 E5
Park Hall Cl CHSW S40 33 F1
Park Hall Gdns CHSW S40 25 F5
Parkhouse Cl CLCR S45 42 D2
Parkland Dr RCH S42 38 C1
Park La CHNE S41 18 B3
Park Rd CHSW S40 3 G7
RCH S42 39 E4
RCH S42 40 D2
Park Rw CLCR S45 43 E2
Park Side
CHNE (off Stand Rd) S41 18 C3
Parkside Vw CHSW S40 17 F4
Park St CHSW S40 34 C1
Park Vw CHNE S41 35 F1
RCH S42 39 H4
STV/CWN S43 14 B2
Parwich Cl CHSW S40 17 E5
Parwich Rd RCH S42 39 H5
Paton Gv STV/CWN S43 19 F2
Patterdale Cl DRON S18 4 C3
Pattison St BSVR S44 22 D4
Pavilion Cl STV/CWN S43 14 A5
Paxton Rd CHNE S41 19 E5
Peak Pl STV/CWN S43 20 D3
Peak Vw STV/CWN S43 13 H2
Peak View Rd CHSW S40 2 A2
Pearce La RCH S42 33 G5
Pearsons Cft CHSW S40 17 G4
Peartree Av RCH S42 34 A5
Pear Tree Cl STV/CWN S43 20 A2
Peggars Cl STV/CWN S43 13 F1
Pembroke Cl CHSW * S40 25 G4
Pembroke Rd DRON S18 5 E4
Penistone Gdns CLCR S45 43 F4
Penmore Cl CHNE S41 27 E4
Penmore Gdns CHNE S41 27 E5
Penmore La CHNE S41 27 E5
Penmore St CHNE S41 27 E5
Penncroft Dr CLCR S45 43 F3
Penncroft La CLCR S45 43 F4
Pennine Wy CHSW S40 2 A2
RCH S42 35 H5
Pennywell Dr RCH S42 32 B1
Penrose Crs BSVR S44 28 D2
Pentland Cl CHSW S40 17 G5
Pentland Rd DRON S18 4 B3
Peterdale Cl STV/CWN S43 19 G2
Peterdale Rd STV/CWN S43 19 G2
Peter More Hl WRKS S80 15 G4
Peters Av CLCR S45 42 D2
Pettyclose La CHNE S41 19 F5
Pevensey Av CHNE S41 18 A4
Peveril Rd BSVR S44 30 D2
CHNE S41 18 B3
Pewit Cl RCH S42 40 D3
Piccadilly CHNE S41 3 K7
Piccadilly Rd CHNE S41 3 K7
Pickton Cl CHSW S40 25 H3
Pike Cl CHSW S40 17 F5
Pilsley Rd CLCR S45 43 F3
Pindale Av STV/CWN S43 20 C3
Pine St STV/CWN S43 20 A2
Pine Vw CHSW S40 25 F2
CLCR S45 43 G4
Pinfold Cl RCH S42 24 C5
Pingle Gra STV/CWN S43 19 G3
Piper Av CLCR S45 43 G2
Piper La RCH S42 24 C2
Pitch Cl STV/CWN S43 14 A5
Plantation Cl WRKS S80 15 G2
Pleasant Pl
CHSW (off Barker La) S40 2 B6
Plover Wy STV/CWN S43 27 H2
Pocknedge La RCH S42 24 B4
Polyfields La BSVR S44 31 F5
Pond La RCH S42 34 A4
RCH S42 39 F3
Pond St CHSW S40 26 C3
Pondwell Dr STV/CWN S43 19 H3
Poolsbrook Av STV/CWN S43 21 G2
Poolsbrook Crs STV/CWN S43 21 G2
Poolsbrook Rd BSVR S44 21 G4
Poolsbrook Sq STV/CWN S43 21 G2
Poolsbrook Vw STV/CWN S43 21 G2
Poplar Av CHSW S40 25 F4
Poplar Cl DRON S18 5 G5
Poplar Pl
CHNE (off St Johns Rd) S41 18 B2
The Poplars
RCH (off Main Rd) S42 16 D2
Porter St STV/CWN S43 11 E5
Portland Av BSVR S44 31 F4
Portland Crs BSVR S44 31 F4
Portland St STV/CWN S43 14 C3
WRKS S80 15 H1
Postmans La RCH S42 36 B4
Potters Cl CHNE S41 8 D5
Pottery La East CHNE S41 18 D2
Pottery La West CHNE S41 18 C3
Prestwold Wy CHNE S41 35 E1
Pretoria St BSVR S44 22 D4
Priestfield Gdns CHSW S40 17 F3
Princess Pl CLCR S45 43 E4
Princess Rd DRON S18 5 E2
Princess St CHNE S41 3 F3
STV/CWN S43 19 H1
Private Dr STV/CWN S43 20 A2
Prospect Rd CHNE S41 8 B5
DRON S18 5 G1
Prospect Ter CHSW S40 2 D3
Pullman Cl STV/CWN S43 11 F4
Pump Houses
STV/CWN (off Norbriggs Rd) S43 12 A5
Purbeck Av CHSW S40 2 A3
Pynot Rd CHNE S41 8 D5

Q

Quantock Wy CHSW S40 17 F5
Quarry Bank Rd CHNE S41 27 E3
Quarry La CHSW S40 25 G3
Quarry Rd BSVR S44 31 E2
Queen Mary Rd CHSW S40 25 F4
Queen St CHSW S40 3 F4
CLCR S45 43 E4
STV/CWN S43 19 H1
STV/CWN S43 20 D2
Queen St North CHNE S41 18 C2
Queensway RCH S42 41 E2
Queen Victoria Rd RCH S42 39 E2
Quoit Gn DRON S18 5 F3
Quorn Dr CHSW S40 17 E5

R

Racecourse Mt CHNE S41 18 B2
Racecourse Rd CHNE S41 18 B2
Racecourse Rd East CHNE S41 18 D2
Railway Ter
CHNE (off Storforth La) S41 34 D1
Ralph Rd STV/CWN S43 11 G5
Ramper Av STV/CWN S43 14 A5
Ramsey Av CHSW S40 25 H4
Ramshaw Cl CHSW S40 17 G3
Ramshaw Rd DRON S18 8 A1
Raneld Mt CHSW S40 25 G5
Ranmoor Cl CHNE * S41 27 E5
Ravensdale Cl STV/CWN S43 20 C4
Ravensdale Rd DRON S18 4 A3
Ravenswood Rd RCH S42 17 E5
Rayleigh Av STV/CWN S43 19 F2
Recreation Cl STV/CWN S43 14 A3
Recreation Rd STV/CWN S43 19 H5
Rectory Cl BSVR S44 29 G2
Rectory Dr RCH S42 33 H4
Rectory Rd BSVR S44 29 G1
STV/CWN S43 11 E5
STV/CWN S43 14 A3
Redacre Cl BSVR S44 31 G3
Redbrook Av CHNE S41 26 D5
Redfern St RCH S42 39 E4
Redgrove Wy CHSW S40 25 G5
Redhouse Cl STV/CWN S43 9 F3
Red La CHNE S41 19 E1
Rednall Cl CHSW S40 17 E5
Redvers Buller Rd CHSW S40 26 C4
Redwood Cl STV/CWN S43 20 A2
Regent St STV/CWN S43 13 H3
Rembrandt Dr DRON S18 4 C3
Renishaw Rd STV/CWN S43 12 A2
Repton Cl CHSW S40 17 E5
Repton Pl DRON S18 4 A3
Reservoir Ter CHSW S40 2 D3
Reynolds Cl DRON S18 4 C4
Rhodes Av CHNE S41 2 D1
Rhodesia Rd CHSW S40 25 F3
Riber Cl STV/CWN S43 20 C5
Riber Crs CLCR S45 42 D1
Riber Ter CHSW S40 26 A3
Richmond Cl CHSW S40 26 A5
Riddings Cft CHSW S40 17 G4
Ridd Wy RCH S42 34 C5
Ridgedale Rd BSVR S44 31 E4
Ridgeway DRON S18 5 H1
STV/CWN S43 14 B4
Ridgeway Av BSVR S44 31 F3
Ridgeway West STV/CWN S43 14 A5
Riggotts Wy RCH S42 16 C3
Ringer La STV/CWN S43 14 A4
Ringer Wy STV/CWN S43 14 A4
Ringwood Av CHNE S41 18 A3
STV/CWN S43 20 C2
Ringwood Rd STV/CWN S43 19 H2
Ringwood Vw STV/CWN S43 19 H3
Riverdale Pk
STV/CWN (off Bent La) S43 11 G4
Riverside Crs RCH S42 32 B1
Riverside Wy BSVR S44 30 C3
River Vw
CHSW (off Derby Rd) S40 26 D4
Robert Cl DRON S18 8 A2
Robertson's Av BSVR S44 29 G1
Robincroft CHSW S40 34 B1
Robincroft Rd RCH S42 33 H4
Rock Crs CLCR S45 42 C2
Rockingham Cl CHSW S40 25 G2
DRON S18 4 A3
Rock La RCH S42 37 E2
Rockley Cl CHSW S40 34 B1
Rockside
STV/CWN (off North Rd) S43 14 A3
Rodge Cft CHNE S41 8 C4
Rodsley Cl CHSW S40 17 F5
Roecar Cl CHNE S41 8 D5
Romeley Crs STV/CWN S43 13 H4
Romney Dr DRON S18 4 C3
Rood La STV/CWN S43
Rose Av BSVR S44
STV/CWN S43
Rose Crs STV/CWN S43
Rosedale Av CHSW S40
Rosedale Vw CHSW S40
Rose Garth Cl CHNE S41
Rose Hl CHSW S40
Rosehill Ct BSVR S44
Rose Hl East CHSW S40
Rose Hl West CHSW S40
Rose Wood Cl CHNE S41
Rosling Wy BSVR S44
Rossendale Cl CHSW S40
Roston Cl DRON S18
Rothay Cl DRON S18
Rother Av STV/CWN S43
Rother Cl CHSW S40
Rother Cft RCH S42
Rotherham Rd STV/CWN S43
Rothervale Rd CHSW S40
Rother Wy CHNE S41
Rothey Gv RCH S42
Rowan Cl WRKS S80
Rowan Rd STV/CWN S43
Rowsley Crs STV/CWN S43
Rubens Cl DRON S18
Rufford Cl CHSW S40
Rushen Mt RCH S42
The Rusk STV/CWN * S43
Russell Gdns RCH S42
Ruston Cl CHSW S40
Rutland Av BSVR S44
Rutland Rd CHSW S40
Rutland St CHNE S41
Rydal Cl DRON S18
Rydal Crs CHNE S41
Rydal Wy CLCR S45
Rye Crs CLCR S45
Rye Flatt La CHSW S40
Ryehill Av CHSW S40
Rykneld Ct CLCR S45
Rykneld Ri RCH S42

S

Sackville Cl CHSW S40
St Albans Cl RCH S42
St Andrews Ri CHSW * S40
St Augustines Av CHSW S40
St Augustines Dr CHSW S40
St Augustines Mt CHSW S40
St Augustines Ri CHSW S40
St Augustines Rd CHSW S40
St David's Ri CHSW S40
St Giles Cl CHSW S40
St Helen's Cl CHNE S41
St Helen's St CHNE S41
St James Cl CHNE * S41
St Johns Cl CHSW S40
St John's Crs STV/CWN S43
St John's Mt CHNE S41
St Johns Pl STV/CWN S43
St John's Rd CHNE * S41
STV/CWN S43
St Lawrence Av BSVR S44
St Lawrence Rd RCH S42
St Lawrence Vw WRKS S80
St Margaret's Dr CHSW S40
St Mark's Rd CHSW S40
St Martins Cl CHSW S40
St Mary's Ga CHNE S41
St Pauls Av CHNE S41
St Peters Cl BSVR S44
St Philip's Dr CHNE S41
St Thomas' St CHSW S40
Salcey Sq CHSW S40
Sales Av RCH S42
Salisbury Av CHNE S41
DRON S18
Salisbury Crs CHNE S41
Salisbury Rd DRON S18
Saltergate CHSW S40
Salvin Crs STV/CWN S43
Sandhills Rd BSVR S44
Sandiway CHSW S40
Sandringham Cl STV/CWN S43
Sandstone Av CHSW S40
Sandy Cl WRKS S80
Sandy La WRKS S80
Sanforth St CHNE S41
Scarsdale Cl DRON S18
Scarsdale Crs STV/CWN S43
Scarsdale Cross DRON S18
Scarsdale Rd CHNE S41
DRON S18

St *BSVR* S44......30 C5
ard La *CHSW* S40 ......2 C6
 BSVR S44......28 D2
18......5 E3
d *CHNE* S41 ......18 C3
 St *WRKS* S80......15 H1
RCH S42......35 G4
 Dr *CHNE* S41......35 E1
Av *BSVR* S44......31 E4
 Av *RCH* S42......40 D3
 Crs *CHNE* S41......17 H3
oor Cl *CHSW* S40......25 F1
CHSW S40......25 G5
Rd *CHNE* S41......3 F1
t *STV/CWN* S43......19 F2
t *BSVR* S44......31 G5
 RCH S42......34 D4
rs *RCH* S42......43 H1
 La *STV/CWN* S43......12 A5
ury Av *CHSW* S40 ......2 B5
Cl *CLCR* S45......43 G2
eare Crs *DRON* S18......5 G4
eare St *RCH* S42......35 G5
2......40 D2
mbles *CHSW* S40......3 H6
ck Pl *STV/CWN* S43......12 A3
CHSW S40......17 G5
Rw *CHSW* S40......2 A7
CHNE S41......18 C2
2......40 D2
Cl *DRON* S18......4 C3
 Dr *DRON* S18......4 C3
 Wy *DRON* S18......4 C3
I Rd *CHNE* S41......3 H1
 S18......5 E4
 S18......8 A3
WN S43......14 D4
 Rd *CHSW* S40......17 F5
 Dr *DRON* S18......5 G5
St *RCH* S42......40 D2
St *CHSW* S40......2 B7
arne Av *CHNE* S41......18 A2
od Rd *DRON* S18......4 B3
od St *BSVR* S44......30 C5
 S40......26 D4
l Av *STV/CWN* S43......20 B3
 BSVR S44......37 F4
ks Rd *DRON* S18......5 G2
I St *CHNE* S41......3 H3
CHNE S40......17 F5
 RCH S42......32 B1
rs Drift *STV/CWN* S43......13 F1
wood Rd *BSVR* S44......22 D4
ngs *STV/CWN* S43......14 A3
Cl *CHSW* S40......17 G5
ale Cl *CHNE* S41......18 A1
t *CHNE* S41......9 E4
Av *CHSW* S40......26 B4
e Dr *CHSW* S40......26 D5
h Cl *CHNE* S41......17 H2
w Cl *CHNE* S41......17 H4
 St *WRKS* S80......15 F5
 BSVR S44......41 E1
 S40......25 F2
 ECK/KIL S21......9 F1
t *CLCR* S45......43 E3
HI *STV/CWN* S43 ......13 G3
 Vw *STV/CWN* S43 ......13 G2
View Rd *STV/CWN* S43 ......13 F1
ey Wood Cl *DRON* S18 ......7 G4
nghouse La *DRON* S18 ......6 C4
Av *STV/CWN* S43......20 B3
ne *CHNE* S41......27 F4
eld Av *CHNE* S41......35 E1
on Av *BSVR* S44......31 F4
 Av *CLCR* S45......43 E2
Cft *DRON* S18......4 A2
Pl *RCH* S42......39 H1
HI *DRON* S18......5 E1
hill Cl *DRON* S18......5 E1
hill Crs *DRON* S18......5 E1
Hill Dr *DRON* S18......5 F1
Hill La *DRON* S18......5 E2
on Cl *DRON* S18......4 A3
Cl *RCH* S42......32 B1
r La *DRON* S18......5 F2
sall Cl *CHSW* S40......25 E4
sall La *CHSW* S40......25 E4
sall Park Rd *CHSW* S40......25 E4
sall Willows *CHSW* S40......25 E4
sby Av *CHSW* S40......33 F1
set Dr *STV/CWN* S43......19 H2
y St *CHSW* S40......3 G6
Cl *DRON* S18......8 A1
cote Dr *DRON* S18......4 B3
rs *BSVR* S44......21 G5

BSVR S44......31 F4
Southdown Av *CHSW* S40......25 G1
Southend *RCH* S42......39 H1
Southfield Av *CHNE* S41......35 F2
Southfield Cl *WRKS* S80......15 H2
Southfield Dr *DRON* S18......5 G4
Southfield Mt *DRON* S18......5 G4
Southfields *STV/CWN* S43......14 B4
Southgate Crs *STV/CWN* S43......14 B2
Southgate Wy *STV/CWN* S43......10 B3
South Lodge Ct *CHSW* S40......25 F2
Southmoor Cl *STV/CWN* S43......27 H1
South Pl *CHSW* S40......3 H7
South St *CHSW* S40......3 H7
South St North *STV/CWN* S43......9 F3
South Vw *WRKS* S80......15 H2
Southwood Av *DRON* S18......5 E5
Southwood Dr *STV/CWN* S43......14 B4
Spa La *CHNE* S41......3 J6
Speighthill Crs *RCH* S42......34 A4
Spencer Av *STV/CWN* S43......11 H5
Spencer St *BSVR* S44......30 D5
CHSW S40......3 G4
Spital Brook Cl *CHNE* S41......27 E4
Spital Gdns *CHNE* S41......27 E4
Spital La *CHNE* S41......3 K7
Spittal Gn *BSVR* S44......31 E5
Spring Bank Rd *CHSW* S40......2 E5
Springfield Av *CHSW* S40......2 B5
Springfield Cl *STV/CWN* S43......14 A4
Springfield Cottages
 RCH (off Hepthorne La) S42......39 H5
Springfield Crs *BSVR* S44......30 D2
Springfield Rd *DRON* S18......6 B4
 RCH S42......40 D3
Spring House Cl *RCH* S42......16 D5
Spring Pl
 CHSW (off Saltergate) S40......3 G5
Springvale Cl *CLCR* S45......43 F4
Springvale Rd *CLCR* S45......43 F4
Spring Vale Rd *STV/CWN* S43......19 G2
Spring Wood Cl *CHNE* S41......17 G2
Springwood Ct
 STV/CWN (off Church Wk) S43 ......9 F3
Springwood St *RCH* S42......36 B4
The Square *WRKS* S80......15 H1
Stables Ct *BSVR* S44......31 G4
Stafford Cl *DRON* S18......4 A2
Stainsby Cl *BSVR* S44......41 F2
Stanage Wy *RCH* S42......16 D5
Stand Pk
 CHNE (off Sheffield Rd) S41......18 C3
Stand Rd *CHNE* S41......18 B3
Stanford Rd *DRON* S18......4 A3
Stanford Wy *CHSW* S40......25 F5
Stanley Av *STV/CWN* S43......20 B3
Stanley St *CHNE* S41......26 D3
Stanwood Dr *CHSW* S40......25 F5
Statham Av *RCH* S42......39 E3
Station La *CHNE* S41......8 C5
Station New Rd *RCH* S42......39 F4
Station Rd *BSVR* S44......30 C3
 CHNE S41......3 J6
 CHNE S41......18 C1
 RCH S42......39 G5
 STV/CWN S43......10 B4
 STV/CWN S43......14 A3
 STV/CWN S43......19 E2
 STV/CWN S43......20 A1
Staveley Rd *BSVR* S44......29 E1
 STV/CWN S43......21 G2
Steele Av *STV/CWN* S43......20 B4
Steel La *BSVR* S44......31 F3
Steeping Cl *STV/CWN* S43......19 G2
Steep La *RCH* S42......33 E4
Steeplegate *CHSW* S40......3 H6
Stephenson Pl *CHNE* * S41......3 H6
 CHSW S40......3 H6
 CLCR S45......42 C2
Stephenson Rd *STV/CWN* S43......21 E1
Sterland St *CHSW* S40......2 D6
Sterry Cl *STV/CWN* S43......14 A5
Stillman Cl *CHNE* S41......27 E5
Stockley Vw *BSVR* S44......31 F5
Stollard St *CLCR* S45......43 F2
Stone Cl *DRON* S18......5 G1
Stonegravels La *CHNE* S41......3 H1
Stoneholes Dr *CLCR* S45......43 G4
Stone La *STV/CWN* S43......9 F3
Stonelow Crs *DRON* S18......5 H2
Stonelow Rd *DRON* S18......5 F2
Stone Rw *CHSW* S40......2 B7
 RCH (off Nethermoor Rd) S42......39 E4
Stoneycroft La *RCH* S42......33 E4
Stoops St *CHSW* S40......17 H4
Storforth La *CHNE* S41......35 E1
 CHSW S40......34 C1

Storforth Lane Ter *CHNE* S41......26 D5
Storrs Rd *CHSW* S40......25 F3
Stour Cl *STV/CWN* S43......19 G2
Stradbroke Ri *CHSW* S40......25 G5
Stratton Rd *BSVR* S44......31 E3
Stretton Rd *CLCR* S45......43 E4
The Stride
 CHSW (off Birchwood Crs) S40 ......34 B1
Stuart Cl *CHNE* S41......18 D4
Stubbing Rd *CHSW* S40......34 B1
Stubley Cl *DRON* S18......4 C2
Stubley Cft *DRON* S18......4 B2
Stubley Dr *DRON* S18......4 C2
Stubley Hollow *DRON* S18......4 C2
Stubley La *DRON* S18......4 B2
Stubley Pl *DRON* S18......4 C2
Sudbury Cl *CHSW* S40......17 F5
Sudhall Cl *CHNE* S41......17 H2
Summerfield Crs *STV/CWN* S43......19 G2
Summerfield Rd *CHSW* S40......26 B4
 DRON S18......5 F1
Summerskill Gn *STV/CWN* S43......20 C3
Summerwood La *DRON* S18......4 D1
Summerwood Pl *DRON* S18......4 D2
Sunningdale Cl *CHSW* S40......26 A5
Sunningdale Ri *CHSW* S40......25 G5
Sunny Brook Cl *STV/CWN* S43......14 A4
Sunny Springs *CHNE* S41......3 H3
Sutton Crs *STV/CWN* S43......20 C3
Sutton Hall Rd *BSVR* S44......30 C5
Sutton La *BSVR* S44......31 E5
 BSVR S44......37 F1
Sutton Vw *BSVR* S44......31 F5
Swaddale Av *CHNE* S41......18 D4
Swaddale Cl *CHNE* S41......18 D4
Swanwick St *CHNE* S41......8 C5
Swathwick Cl *RCH* S42......34 A4
Swathwick La *RCH* S42......33 G4
Swinscoe Wy *RCH* S42......16 D5
Swithland *CHNE* S41......35 E1
Sycamore Av *CHSW* S40......26 A4
 DRON S18......5 E1
 WRKS S80......15 G5
Sycamore Cl *BSVR* S44......31 G3
Sycamore Dr *CHNE* S41......27 F2
Sycamore St *STV/CWN* S43......13 F1
 STV/CWN S43......20 A1
Sycamore Rd *STV/CWN* S43......19 H1
Sydney St *CHSW* S40......2 C6
Sylvan Cl *CHNE* S41......26 D4
Sylvan Dr *RCH* S42......38 C5
Sylvia Rd *DRON* S18......7 H2

T

Taddington Rd *CHSW* * S40......17 F5
Talbot Crs *CHNE* S41......35 F1
Talbot St *CHNE* S41......35 F1
Tallys End *STV/CWN* S43......13 E1
Tansley Dr *CHSW* S40......17 E5
Tansley Rd *RCH* S42......43 H1
Tansley Wy *STV/CWN* S43......20 C4
Tap La *CHSW* S40......2 D6
Tapton La *CHNE* S41......3 J5
Tapton Lock HI *CHNE* S41......18 D4
Tapton Ter *CHNE* S41......3 K4
Tapton V *CHNE* S41......19 E5
Tapton View Rd *CHNE* S41......1 D2
Tapton Wy *STV/CWN* S43......27 H1
Tay Cl *DRON* S18......4 B2
Taylor Crs *CHNE* S41......27 F4
Telford Crs *STV/CWN* S43......11 F5
Tennyson Av *CHSW* S40......3 F5
Tennyson St *RCH* S42......40 D2
Tennyson Wy *RCH* S42......35 G5
Thanet St *CLCR* S45......43 E3
Theatre La *CHNE* S41......3 J5
Thirlmere Dr *DRON* S18......5 E2
Thirlmere Rd *CHNE* S41......17 G3
Thompson Cl *CHNE* S41......18 C2
Thompson St *CHNE* S41......18 C2
Thoresby Av *STV/CWN* S43......14 C3
Thoresby Pl *STV/CWN* * S43......20 C4
Thornbridge Crs *CHSW* S40......34 B2
Thorndene Cl *CHNE* S41......18 A4
Thorndon Wy *CHSW* S40......25 G5
Thornfield Av *CHSW* S40......24 D1
Thornfield Av *CHSW* S40......25 F5
Thornfield Vls
 BSVR (off Chesterfield Rd) S44 ......22 D4
Thornton Pl *DRON* S18......4 A3
Thorpe Av *WRKS* S80......15 H1
Thorpe Cl *CHNE* S41......18 B2
Tibshelf Rd *RCH* S42......40 D4
Tideswell Cl *STV/CWN* S43......20 B2
Tissington Cl *CHSW* S40......17 F5

Titchfield St *WRKS* S80......15 H1
Toc H Yd
 CHSW (off Old Rd) S40......2 B7
Tollbridge Rd *STV/CWN* S43......11 H5
Tom La *BSVR* S44......21 F5
Tontine Rd *CHSW* S40......3 G7
Top Pingle Cl *STV/CWN* S43......19 G3
Top Rd *BSVR* S44......28 A2
Torrani Wy *RCH* S42......39 H4
Totley Mt *STV/CWN* S43......19 F2
Tower Crs *BSVR* S44......31 F5
Town End *BSVR* S44......31 E3
Traffic Ter
 CHNE (off Storforth La) S41......34 D1
 STV/CWN S43......10 B3
Tranmere Av *CLCR* S45......43 F3
Trans Pennine Trail
 STV/CWN S43......11 F4
Treeneuk Cl *CHSW* S40......25 F1
Trent Gv *DRON* S18......5 F1
Trinity Cl *CHNE* S41......3 F3
Troon Cl *CHSW* S40......25 H4
Troughbrook Rd *STV/CWN* S43......20 B1
Tudor St *STV/CWN* S43......11 F5
Tunstall Gn *CHSW* S40......25 H4
Tunstall Wy *CHSW* S40......25 H4
Tupton Wy *RCH* S42......40 D2
Turnberry Cl *CHSW* S40......25 G5
Turnbull Cl *CHSW* S40......26 B4
Turner Cl *DRON* S18......4 D3
Turner Dr *STV/CWN* S43......20 B3
Turnoaks La *CHSW* S40......34 C1
Tylney Rd *CHSW* S40......33 F1

U

Ullswater Cl *DRON* S18......4 C2
Ullswater Dr *DRON* S18......4 C3
Ullswater Pl *DRON* S18......4 C2
Ulverston Rd *CHNE* S41......17 H3
Underhill Rd *STV/CWN* S43......13 F1
Union Wk
 CHSW (off Saltergate) S40......3 G5
Unstone-Dronfield By-Pass
 DRON S18......4 D1
Unstone HI *DRON* S18......5 H4
Unstone Rd *DRON* S18......8 B2
Upland Ri *CHSW* S40......25 H4
Upper Croft *STV/CWN* S43......19 G3
Upper Mantle Cl *CLCR* S45......43 E2
Upper Moor St *CHSW* * S40......25 F3
Upper Newbold Cl *CHSW* S40......17 F3
Upper School La *DRON* S18......5 E3
Upwood Cl *STV/CWN* S43......17 E5

V

Vale Cl *BSVR* S44......31 E4
 DRON S18......5 F3
Valley Crs *CHNE* S41......27 E3
Valley Ri *DRON* S18......6 B4
Valley Rd *BSVR* S44......31 E5
 CHNE S41......27 E3
 CLCR S45......42 C2
 DRON S18......6 D4
 STV/CWN S43......12 A3
Valley View Cl *CHNE* S41......35 G1
Venture Wy *CHNE* S41......18 B1
Vernon Ri *RCH* S42......39 H1
Vernon Rd *CHSW* S40......2 B6
Vicarage Cl *BSVR* S44......41 H1
Vicar La *CHSW* S40......3 H6
Victoria Av *STV/CWN* S43......11 F4
Victoria Gv *STV/CWN* S43......19 H5
Victoria Park Rd *STV/CWN* S43......19 H5
Victoria St *BSVR* S44......31 F5
 CHNE S41......3 G4
 DRON S18......4 D2
 STV/CWN S43......19 H1
Victoria St North *CHNE* S41......8 B5
Victoria St West *CHSW* S40......25 G3
Victoria Vls
 CHNE (off Albert St North) S41......18 B2
Villas Rd *BSVR* S44......30 C4
Vincent Crs *CHSW* S40......25 F3
Vincent La *CHSW* S40......25 F3
Vivian St *BSVR* S44......22 D4

W

Wain Av *RCH* S42......40 A4
Walgrove Av *CHSW* S40......25 H4

Index - featured places

athcote Infant School
.41...................................... 18 B2
xton School
S18 .... 5 G2
gg Infant School
S18 .... 4 B3
r Golf Centre
S41 .... 35 G4
r Primary School
2 .... 39 G1
e Shopping Centre
S18 .... 5 F2
ool
S41 .... 27 F3
Golf Club
S18 .... 5 F5
on Industrial Estate
WN S43 .... 11 E3
Hall Community School
S41 .... 35 F1
Primary Infant School
S41 .... 27 E5
Primary Junior School
S41 .... 35 E1
imary School
S44 .... 41 F2
adley Infant School
WN S43 .... 19 H2
Community School
WN S43 .... 13 H3
d Hall Primary School
.... 18 B4
eet Medical Centre
WN S43 .... 11 E5
vood Primary School
.... 20 A1
use School
S41 .... 8 C4
all Primary School
.... 17 F5
ood Business Park
S40 .... 40 C1
ood Industrial Estate
S42 .... 41 F3
vood Industrial Park
S42 .... 40 D2
te Primary School
S45 .... 42 C2
e Park Primary School
S42 .... 34 C4
l Primary School
CWN S43 .... 20 C3
Industrial Estate
CWN S43 .... 21 G3
Industrial Estate
CWN S43 .... 21 F1
l Infant School
V S18 .... 5 F1
College & Health Club
N S40 .... 2 E5

Manor Infant School
STV/CWN S43 .... 19 H5
Market Hall
CHSW S40 .... 3 G6
Mary Swanick Primary School
CHNE S41 .... 8 C4
Meadows Community School
CHNE S41 .... 8 D4
Middlecroft Leisure Centre
STV/CWN S43 .... 20 D3
Netherthorpe School
STV/CWN S43 .... 11 G5
Newbold CE Primary School
CHSW S40 .... 18 A3
Newbold Community School
CHNE S41 .... 17 H4
Newspaper Office
CHNE S41 .... 3 J6
New Whittington
Infant School
CHNE S41 .... 9 F3
New Whittington
Primary School
CHNE S41 .... 9 F4
North Derbyshire
Health Authority
CHSW S40 .... 3 G4
North Derbyshire
Tertiary College
BSVR S44 .... 31 E4
North Derbyshire
Tertiary College
STV/CWN S43 .... 14 A3
Northfield Junior School
DRON S18 .... 5 G1
North Wingfield Infant School
RCH S42 .... 39 H4
North Wingfield Junior School
RCH S42 .... 39 H4
Old Church School
RCH S42 .... 39 H1
Old Hall Junior School
CHSW S40 .... 25 G3
Parkside Community School
CHSW S40 .... 26 B3
The Pavement
Shopping Centre
CHSW S40 .... 3 G6
Pearsons Trading Estate
CHNE S41 .... 18 D1
Peel Centre & CAB
DRON S18 .... 5 E3
Pomegranate Theatre
CHNE S41 .... 3 J6
Portland Works
CHSW S40 .... 26 A3
Queens Park Leisure Centre
CHSW S40 .... 3 F7
Ragged School
CHSW S40 .... 3 G7

Railway Staff Social &
Sports Club
STV/CWN S43 .... 19 H1
Ravenside Retail Park
CHSW S40 .... 3 G7
Revolution House
CHNE S41 .... 8 C4
Rother Junior School
CHSW S40 .... 26 C5
Royal Mail Delivery Office
CHSW S40 .... 2 E7
St Andrews CE Methodist
Aided School
DRON S18 .... 4 B3
St Johns Business Centre
CHNE S41 .... 18 B2
St Josephs Convent School
CHNE S41 .... 3 F4
St Josephs RC Primary School
STV/CWN S43 .... 20 D1
St Marys RC High School
STV/CWN S43 .... 17 G3
St Marys RC Primary School
CHSW S40 .... 3 F4
St Peter & St Paul School
CHNE S41 .... 27 E2
St Peters & St Pauls School
CHNE S41 .... 27 E5
Saltergate Health Centre
CHSW S40 .... 3 G5
Sharley Park Leisure Centre
CLCR S45 .... 43 F2
Sheepbridge Business Centre
CHNE S41 .... 8 A5
Southfield Industrial Estate
WRKS S80 .... 15 H2
Speedwell Industrial Estate
STV/CWN S43 .... 21 E1
Speedwell Infant School
STV/CWN S43 .... 21 E1
Springbank Community Centre
CHSW S40 .... 2 D5
Springwell Community School
STV/CWN S43 .... 20 D3
Station Lane
Industrial Estate
CHNE S41 .... 8 D5
Station Road Industrial Estate
STV/CWN S43 .... 14 A3
Staveley Health Clinic
STV/CWN S43 .... 21 E1
Staveley Junior School
STV/CWN S43 .... 20 D1
Staveley Norbriggs
County Infants School
STV/CWN S43 .... 12 A4
Stonedge Golf Club
CLCR S45 .... 32 B4
Stonelow Junior School
DRON S18 .... 5 G2

Storforth Lane Trading Estate
CHNE S41 .... 26 D5
Tapton Park Golf &
Leisure Centre
CHNE S41 .... 27 E1
Temple Normanton
Primary School
RCH S42 .... 36 C4
Tower Business Park
CLCR S45 .... 42 D2
Town Hall
CHSW S40 .... 3 F6
Tupton Hall School
RCH S42 .... 39 E4
Tupton Primary School
RCH S42 .... 39 E2
Turnoaks Business Park
CHSW S40 .... 34 C2
Vanguard Trading Estate
CHSW S40 .... 34 C1
Walton Holymoorside
Primary School
RCH S42 .... 32 C1
Walton Hospital
CHSW S40 .... 34 A1
Warwick Street
Industrial Estate
CHSW S40 .... 26 D5
Westfield Infant School
CHSW S40 .... 25 F3
Wheatbridge Retail Park
CHSW S40 .... 2 E7
Whitecotes Primary School
CHSW S40 .... 26 B5
Whittington Medical Centre
CHNE S41 .... 8 C4
Whittington Moor Surgery
CHNE S41 .... 18 D3
William Levick Infant School
DRON S18 .... 4 A2
William Levick Primary School
DRON S18 .... 4 A2
William Rhodes Primary School
CHSW S40 .... 26 A3
Williamthorpe Industrial Park
RCH S42 .... 40 D1
The Winding Wheel Theatre
CHNE S41 .... 3 H5
Woodthorpe CE Primary School
STV/CWN S43 .... 22 A1
Yard Dye Works
RCH S42 .... 32 B2

Notes

Notes

 **AA** **Street by Street** QUESTIONNAIRE

Dear Atlas User
Your comments, opinions and recommendations are very important to us.
So please help us to improve our street atlases by taking a few minutes
to complete this simple questionnaire.

You do NOT need a stamp (unless posted outside the UK). If you do not want to remove this page from your street atlas, then photocopy it or write your answers on a plain sheet of paper.

Send to: The Editor, AA Street by Street, FREEPOST SCE 4598,
Basingstoke RG21 4GY

ABOUT THE ATLAS...

Which city/town/county did you buy?

Are there any features of the atlas or mapping that you find particularly useful?

Is there anything we could have done better?

Why did you choose an AA Street by Street atlas?

Did it meet your expectations?

Exceeded ☐ **Met all** ☐ **Met most** ☐ **Fell below** ☐

Please give your reasons

continued overlea

Where did you buy it?

For what purpose? (please tick all applicable)

To use in your own local area ☐   **To use on business or at work** ☐

Visiting a strange place ☐   **In the car** ☐   **On foot** ☐

Other (please state)

LOCAL KNOWLEDGE...

Local knowledge is invaluable. Whilst every attempt has been made to make the information contained in this atlas as accurate as possible, should you notice any inaccuracies, please detail them below (if necessary, use a blank piece of paper) or e-mail us at *streetbystreet@theAA.com*

ABOUT YOU...

Name (Mr/Mrs/Ms)

Address
                                                            Postcode

Daytime tel no

E-mail address

Which age group are you in?

Under 25 ☐   **25-34** ☐   **35-44** ☐   **45-54** ☐   **55-64** ☐   **65+** ☐

Are you an AA member?   YES ☐   **NO** ☐

Do you have Internet access?   YES ☐   **NO** ☐

Thank you for taking the time to complete this questionnaire. Please send it to us as soon as possible, and remember, you do not need a stamp (unless posted outside the UK).

ML